BEWARE THE PREDATOR
The American's Guide to Personal Security

BEWARE THE PREDATOR
The American's Guide to Personal Security
What YOU need to know!

WARREN D. HOLSTON
Contributing Author Dave White

Foreword by Ambassador Cofer Black

Mockingbird Security

2016

WARREN D. HOLSTON

DEDICATION

To all the brothers and sisters who fight in the shadows.
You are warriors and patriots.

CONTENTS

ACKNOWLEDGMENTS

Special thanks to Ambassador Black for agreeing to be a part of this project. The fact that he would associate his name with my work is humbling.

Mr. Dave White's contributions to the narrative of this book, particularly concerning child safety, has been invaluable in making this work significant to all Americans.

Hat tip to Mike S., (The Dragon), for keeping me honest on communications security.

Thanks to Mary for teaching me the importance of leaving the occasional chewing gum wrapper on the floor to keep the detractors occupied.

WARREN D. HOLSTON

FOREWARD

Our world today is a dangerous place. Predators have always existed in our physical world, and now we must deal with an expanded threat that permeates our virtual existence. Our digital lives converge with family, friends, and business associates and are under unrelenting attack from people trying to acquire our information for nefarious purposes. There are multiple points of intersection between our physical world and our virtual world and vulnerabilities in one can expose vulnerabilities in the other.

How do we deal with multi-faceted and constant threats to our well-being? Through awareness and tradecraft.

Personal tradecraft is not intuitive. Similar to a CIA case officer who must develop a craft and lifestyle to protect human sources, learning the craft of personal security to protect our lives and families from harm is essential. The concepts and techniques defined in *Beware the Predator* help us begin to understand our physical and virtual threats and show us how to develop a defensive posture to deter and defeat predators.

During my career as a CIA operations officer overseas, I watched the rapid evolution of technology and made good operational use of some technical tools at my disposal. After all, technology can make our lives more convenient and efficient. Technology provides insight and expands our knowledge. However, without personal awareness and a commitment to identifying and eliminating threats as they develop, technology is a significant vulnerability. I came to realize that technology is just a tool: it is not the solution to our well-being! The objective is to exist safely while thriving in a world filled with immeasurable dangers.

The predator seeks to outmaneuver their target. For example, a child approaches you, obviously a foreign tourist on a crowded city street. The child is drawing attention to a big piece of white paper held in both hands. How weird! You feel compelled to scrutinize the paper. Are there words on it you can't see? Not to worry, it's just a child. A slight jostling by the passing crowd on the sidewalk and the paper-holding child has disappeared. Later, at the restaurant, you discover your wallet is missing. The paper-holding child was a part of the crime, a momentary distraction. The loss of your wallet could have been avoided.

On a visit to London, I was holding my five-year-old son's hand while walking on a train platform in the "tube" underground subway. A young man approaching us on a mostly deserted platform just "didn't look right." To a predator, my son and I seemed like a target—a father with his young boy unlikely to leave his child to chase a thief. This scene developed into a three-person pickpocket attempt: one thief approaching me from behind to lift my hip-pocket wallet and hand the wallet to a second thief approaching me head-on, who would then slip the wallet to a third thief. Recognizing their intent, I countered their nefarious activity by holding my son with my right hand as I moved my left hand to protect my left hip pocket. With this simple hand movement, while walking and staring ahead, I firmly grabbed the pickpocket's wrist as he attempted to lift my wallet from my pocket. The would-be pickpocket could do no damage as long as I held his wrist. The approaching thief had nothing to receive and froze. The third thief, who was to get the wallet last, looked on in disgust. I commented to them as I kept walking, "You guys need more practice. You would never make it in New York! You are pathetic!"

Recognizing threats as they develop is essential to personal security. The Prevention, Deterrence, Defense strategy described in *Beware the Predator* provides a simple framework for viewing life realistically while identifying vulnerabilities and establishing security measures unique to an individual's life and circumstances. Basic awareness is the foundation of personal security tradecraft. We must begin to see threats as they develop and continually adjust behavior to mitigate them. To achieve this level of awareness, we must critically evaluate our place in our virtual and physical worlds from the standpoint of those who seek to do us harm. Use the checklists in this book as working documents to develop your "personal tradecraft" and to evaluate risk and security. With time, this practice will become second nature.

Ambassador Cofer Black, Washington, D.C.

1 INTRODUCTION

We learned to move freely in anonymity.
There was peace and safety in the darkness.
It is not until the dawn of a new day
when you realize how dark the night was.

Personal awareness is your ability to identify a threat. Personal security tradecraft is your ability to execute your security plan. Personal awareness and security tradecraft are learned skills, skills that only become intuitive with practice and discipline. These skills must be ingrained into your psyche and muscle memory and become a near-automatic response in your daily life to be effective. Lack of awareness and preparation can lead to the exploitation of your identity, intentions, and assets.

On any given day, you can search the Internet and find reports of home invasions, assaults, mass identity theft at national and multinational companies, and workplace violence. These attacks do not even account for the terrorist threat that looms with the rise of ISIS and various extremist organizations.

If you have worked for the government or military in the last 30 years, your personal information is compromised. Hackers have stolen your personal data from places like the Office of Personnel Management and local Veterans Affairs offices. If you are a part of the health care system, a college student, have ever been on federal assistance, or filed a tax return, your personal data is vulnerable. Hackers release stolen personal information on the Internet as a form of terror and harassment or sell it on the Dark Web for profit. Organizations like ISIS and Al-Qaeda use this stolen personal information to target individuals for recruitment or violence. Your participation in life makes you a target and makes you vulnerable.

This book provides practical concepts that you can apply in everyday life to aid both you and your family in identifying and defeating a predator.

You will find there are many security procedures common among chapters such as emergency contacts and self-defense techniques. This commonality is not by accident. The intent is to simplify prevention and defense techniques, so they become second nature and intuitive. Personal awareness must become routine to be effective. Personal awareness and preparation are a lifestyle you must embrace every day, so eventually, they become intuitive in your life without even considering the process. "Life is really simple, but we insist on making it complicated." — Confucius

This book explores personal security from a practical perspective. In our technology-driven world, you typically seek out those technical tools you can use to help protect your data and your life. You can find this information everywhere, but the reality is technology and tools change quickly. The average person has little patience for staying current with the growing complexities of ever-changing computer apps, updates, and online account management. Instead of trying to defeat the onslaught of technology with technology, you can use traditional and practical personal security tradecraft techniques to reduce your exposure and enhance your safety. These concepts are timeless and not dependent upon keeping up with the next generation of encryption, or caring significantly what big box retail store gets hacked. However, you should routinely monitor your life, your online presence, and your financial condition to ensure the techniques you employ are successful and adjust your security plan as necessary. Vigilance is the key!

This book will strengthen your knowledge about:

- Personal awareness and security
- How to protect Personally Identifiable Information
- Communications security
- Vulnerabilities in your everyday life
- Self-defense best practices

2 BASIC TRADECRAFT

You must wield modern technological conveniences with care and purpose. Carelessness and distraction can result in injury and incalculable hardship. Today, you rely heavily on the convenience of technology to simplify your life and improve your efficiency. However, you have also become more vulnerable to exploitation than at any time in history. Predators have easy access to your habits, thoughts, and personal data through marketing research that is for sale or publicly available in social media content. Many people are like the live frog in a slowly boiling pot of water: they fail to realize how much of their privacy they relinquish until they are fully exposed.

Beware the Predator will help you become more aware of subtle changes in your surroundings as you live and conduct business in a real and dangerous world. The techniques defined in this book are simple in concept but require diligence in execution. They will guide you, provoke you to think, and lead you down the path to better personal security preparedness and practices. Take caution; these techniques do not work for everyone all the time, and not every technique is indefinitely viable. You must revise your security posture regularly for it to remain valid.

Your Patterns of Life

It may come as a surprise, but you have a distinct pattern to your life. Your pattern is easy to identify, predict, and exploit. In the spy world, your public or cover life is your in-pattern life. Your private or covert life, the place where you conduct your personal business absent of scrutiny, is your out-of-pattern life. Depending on your risk factors and public exposure, you should consider developing two patterns to your life. The first is your "public" in-pattern life, which the world sees daily. It is unmistakably you. The second is your "private" out-of-pattern life where you can safely conduct your personal and professional business away from watchful eyes. Ideally, your public in-pattern life and your private out-of-pattern persona need to exist both separately and in parallel, with no digital connections. There must be a defined "air gap" between the two patterns; otherwise, there is no way to disassociate the two.

If you are a public figure, politician, or businessperson you may have a social media page for your public image. If you use a smartphone or computer that contains all of your personal or private contacts to access your public social media page, YOU are compromised. The apps inside many social networking sites access the contacts on your phone or computer and associate them with you and your page, all the while exposing your friends and family in the process. Not all social media services or websites collect your personal data but keeping up with which ones do is a daunting task. Having an "air gap" between your two patterns of life helps reduce the need for constant scrutiny of every application and website you use. Determine what you are trying to protect; that goes in your out of pattern life. It is important for you to plan and consider every eventuality. Living within your pattern and protecting yourself is a complicated endeavor. Much like the spy living a cover life, you still must exist in the day-to-day world, and you must learn to anticipate pitfalls as they develop.

Today capitalism creates convenience in business. Companies continuously explore ways to get a better return on their marketing investment. They want to put those items you are most interested in and likely to buy directly in front of you, and not waste time marketing products that you would never consider. These modern marketing techniques are a breach of privacy on an unprecedented scale. The technology developed for these marketing strategies involves collecting and aggregating data. Techniques which predators use to steal and exploit your identity, or otherwise victimize you and your family.

What makes these marketing technologies or techniques so effective? They can discern patterns in your activities and associate your interests and your connections to people and businesses with similar interests. Herein lies the danger: associating or aggregating all of your phone calls, contacts, and emails with particular individuals, businesses, and philosophies. Few filters or software applications exist that block these technologies or the aggregation of the data. For example, if you search for "boots" using your Internet browser, every time you subsequently conduct a search you will get ads in your browser for boots. The same holds true if you are researching a school paper on politics, ideology, and so on. Your browser history links to your searched topics through whichever web browser you use, and this allows you to be exploited. There is no context in Internet searches (e.g., while writing a school paper), so you have no control over how the data are interpreted.

Build a Defensive Posture

To create a sustainable defensive position you must establish concentric rings of increasing levels of security around your life, family, business, and property. This technique provides you with multiple opportunities to identify and defend against would-be predators, and it hardens you as a target, thus making you harder to exploit. Most of the time, predators victimize the weak and the unprotected, so making yourself a difficult or obscure target is paramount.

Your public or outer-most life is where you are the most vulnerable. The closer you get to your home, family, and financial resources, the harder it should be for those outside your circle of trust to access your personal life and information. As an example, if you are like most people, you probably use debit and credit cards routinely. These cards are so convenient and so commonly used you may rarely carry cash. Their use involves the outer-most edge of your life. Every time you use your card to buy groceries, get gas, or order something over the Internet, you not only expose yourself and your data, but you also generate traceable patterns.

You can take several measures to offset the risk and provide a first line of defense to protect your personal information and financial resources. If you use a credit card for day-to-day purchases, for example, set a low credit limit on that card to limit your risk. Use a gas card to buy gas and a separate card to buy groceries and make other purchases. It is also a good idea to use a different card for Internet purchases only. Using this model, it requires greater effort on the part of a predator to get a complete picture of your life from the exploitation of one credit card. Also, compromise of one card does not limit you from using your other cards to fill the gap until you receive a new card and Personal Identification Number (PIN) to replace the compromised card.

Always carry some cash for emergencies in case your cards get locked due to a fraud alert. Most banks, credit card companies, and department stores now employ sophisticated security algorithms that track your in-pattern life and trigger a fraud alert if your card use is inconsistent with your regular routine. In a well-established public pattern of life, others will handle much of your security because it is in their best interest to ensure your safe use of their products.

However, if you entrust someone else to hold your data or your Personally Identifiable Information (PII), you must consider it compromised when developing a security plan. This fact is difficult to comprehend because you like to believe that technology will protect your data as you expose it to the world. In reality, predators continually engage in exploiting and selling technical vulnerabilities such as holes in encryption and tools to collect passwords. **If you assume, from the beginning, that all your PII is compromised, you can develop a security posture that protects you from intrusion instead of falsely believing that you can protect your information from exposure.** While a technologist provides security solutions that revolve around continuous advancements in technology, the Prevention, Deterrence, and Defense (PDD^{TM}) security strategy (detailed in Chapter 3) shows you a different way to think about security while employing classic security tradecraft techniques. You may sometimes use technical solutions in your security plan, but it is important not to rely solely on these technical solutions to keep you safe.

Keep It Simple!

Simplicity is the rule. A system with many moving parts, or significant complexity, is always more vulnerable. Complexity creates risk and exposes your vulnerabilities. As you examine your risk areas, try to view your vulnerabilities and your proposed security plan in as simple a manner as possible to achieve your objectives. Keep in mind that "complexity" does not equal security and "simplicity" does not equal risk.

Having a home alarm system, for example, is a prudent component of your security plan. Alarm technology is mature, reliable, and will earn you a discount with most homeowner insurance carriers. If you install a home alarm system, <u>and</u> you post the alarm company sign conspicuously in front of your home or your apartment window you will deter the majority of burglars. The corollary is, when you spend the money to buy a good security system, you lose the deterrence effect and are more likely to be targeted if you <u>do not</u> post the sign so it can be seen. In fact, the mere act of displaying the security company's sign is a significant deterrent in itself.

The more complicated the security apparatus, the higher the probability of failure. Why? Because as you add more pieces to your security system or plan, you are adding more potential points of failure. You must determine what you are trying to protect and focus on that as your objective. Do not invest in a pneumatic nail driver, with all the hoses and tanks and compressors that can fail, when a claw hammer will do.

3 PDD™ SECURITY CONCEPT

How objective are you when assessing your threat vulnerability? You no doubt believe you are providing a safe environment for yourself and your family, but you may be too close to the vulnerability to see it objectively. In many cases, you may have created a false sense of security for yourself and your family not a truly objective view of reality. What you should explore is the difference between <u>feeling</u> secure and <u>being</u> secure. **It is important to feel secure, but it is more important to be secure!**

The Prevention, Deterrence, and Defense PDD™ concept can help you objectively define your security posture by visualizing concentric rings of ever-increasing security around your life and family. As you get closer to home, and those things you value, you must increase your protection, although it is often difficult to organize something so complex. The PDD™ concept helps you organize your thoughts based on an objective assessment of your life. PDD™ is a framework for you to use in developing your security strategy. You should apply the PDD™ process to every aspect of your life, whether or not this book has addressed your particular circumstances.

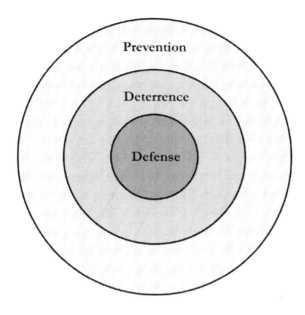

The graphic illustrates the PDD™ concept. Imagine you are at the center of the graphic. The objective is to develop a security posture in which you have multiple opportunities to identify a predator's attack on you or your family before you have to mount a defense. Think of it as a virtual barrier around your life.

Prevention is the outer-most area of your life where you interact with others, give out your PII, and live in the real world. In this area people, businesses, and predators drift in and out through the ordinary course of your life. The objective is to look at the outer-most edge of your life and interactions and identify those things you can do to prevent yourself from becoming a target as the world drifts in and out around you. You encounter predators in your everyday life, but when the predator sees your outer-most public life, he should immediately spot the first barrier to entry: a hard target that presents a low probability of success if attacked.

Deterrence is the secondary barrier around your life. In spite of your efforts at prevention, you may attract the attention of a predator at some point. In the Deterrence phase, you enact those procedures or actions that discourage a predator from continuing to pursue you as a target. If these measures were fences around our lives, the outer fence would be a decorative fence with an alarm company sign that shows we are marking our territory although it is still porous. The secondary fence, or Deterrence phase, would be a chain-link fence with a vicious dog patrolling the interior; visible to a predator. Finally, the third fence is the last barrier to your life where you mount your defense and fight or die. At this point, the predator has identified you as a target, mounted an assault whether physical or virtual, and is now inside your life threatening you, your assets, and your family. This is where you mount a violent defense.

Defense is your inner-most area of security. Whether a predator assaults you physically or exploits your data virtually, you should prepare for an immediate and violent defense. An attack can occur against your data in the blink of an eye just as a physical attack can happen without warning. In developing your defensive posture, you must think about it in terms of urgency. Once the predator is inside the second fence or your area of deterrence, you must take immediate action to minimize the damage and to survive.

.

4 PERSONAL VULNERABILITY ASSESSMENT

Developing a good security plan boils down to employing simple processes that can be applied to any aspect of your life. Our intent is to help you:

1. Determine where you are vulnerable

2. Develop your security strategy

Once you establish the critical thinking, knowledge, and skills you need for your personal security, you can then:

- Make informed decisions

- Accept risk as appropriate

- Mitigate risk where possible

DETERMINING WHERE YOU ARE VULNERABLE

Not everyone has the same risks, so it is important to **modify the provided concepts as appropriate to your circumstances. The intent is NOT to create a rigid list but to give you a decision-making process to apply to your life and family as your circumstances change over time.**

Before developing a good security strategy, you must determine where you are vulnerable. You need to identify the aspects of your life that are exposed to others, both publicly and privately. Any exposure carries risk, but unless you want to live like a hermit, some exposure is inevitable. This chapter helps you identify your vulnerabilities and evaluate your risk of exposure. Later, you will develop your security strategy. You may make a conscious decision to accept certain risks, but it should be a conscious, informed decision and not one borne from complacency or ignorance of the facts.

Look at your life holistically. Our concepts of security awareness and tradecraft will help you address common risk areas and give you the thought processes to address those risk areas specific to your life.

Break down your life into the five broad areas of vulnerability listed below. Then, further dissect each of these areas depending on the complexity of your life.

- Personally Identifiable Information (PII)
- Computers, Phones, and Social Media
- Vulnerabilities in the Home
- Vulnerabilities outside the Home
- Child Safety

In each of these broad areas of vulnerability, you must determine:

1. **Where you are vulnerable to attack, both physical and virtual, and**
2. **What you are vulnerable to**

Using your home as an example, you can use the following checklist as the foundation for identifying:

Those areas that are vulnerable to attack around the home

- Your profile
- Garbage

- Mail
- Wi-Fi
- Your guns and valuables
- Your children or family members
- _____

Those things that you are vulnerable to around the home

- Home invasion
- Fire
- Medical emergency
- Domestic help
- Heavy neighborhood crime
- Natural Disaster
- _____

Once you identify vulnerabilities in a given area of your life, you must develop a security plan consistent with your risk and resources.

DEVELOPING YOUR SECURITY STRATEGY

Sometimes you may determine that even though there is a danger of exploitability, the risk is so small it is not cost-effective to address in your security plan. However, if you determine there is a significant danger of exploitability, you should identify your vulnerabilities and assess your risks so you can develop an effective security plan.

Take a logical approach when you identify both your weaknesses and risks. For example, what do you know about home security cameras? At a minimum, you have to understand what to monitor, where to place the cameras, and how to use the data you collect with the cameras. Otherwise, you will likely waste money and develop a false sense of security, while remaining vulnerable.

Another area of concern involves owning and carrying a firearm. If you are a law-abiding citizen, you can buy a gun, get a concealed weapons permit in many states, and legally carry a weapon for self-defense. Acquiring the weapon and getting the permit are easy. However, before acting, you should objectively look at your life, personality, and background to determine whether carrying a weapon or having a weapon in the home may be more of a risk than an asset. If you are not adequately trained and comfortable using a gun, then under the stress of an emergency your reactions could expose you to greater legal liability in addition to the risk of physical harm. Consider other self-defense techniques once you assess your risk, your individual tolerance, and your personal capabilities.

You should start with a checklist when you begin to develop your security plan. Concentrate on those areas where you can make reasonable adjustments to enhance your security posture within your personal and financial resources.

Simple changes to your habits and lifestyle can make a significant impact on your security posture. For example, appearing to be a difficult target is often as effective as employing an elaborate security plan. When a predator is considering you as a potential target, you must appear strong and capable of deterring the predator. If the predator perceives you as a strong, confident persona, aware of your surroundings and poised to take defensive action at a moment's notice, then you have introduced doubts about a successful outcome in the predator's calculations.

Whether physical or virtual, a strong, confident persona will often cause a predator to pass you by just because easier targets require less effort and offer the predator a higher probability of success. In this case, we will use a porcupine to illustrate our point. While a porcupine is small and usually alone, predators infrequently attack them because the porcupine can inflict so much pain even when it loses. Such an encounter offers the predator a low-probability of success and introduces the idea, in the predator's mind, that the cost is not worth the benefit. Similarly, you want to build up your personal security defenses so that when the predator sees you, he sees a porcupine. Be the porcupine!

5 PERSONALLY IDENTIFIABLE INFORMATION

Personally Identifiable Information, or PII, is any information used to identify you. To put it another way, PII is information that someone can use to steal your identity.

How does identity theft work? It is typically a two-step process. The people aggregating or stealing your PII are not usually the same people stealing your identity. They are the data brokers who enable identity theft. They sell identity packages containing complete sets of an identity's PII on an exchange where identity thieves use each persona to obtain credit, buy goods, and then convert them to cash. PII data needed to clone your identity includes:

- Birth date and place of birth
- Social Security number
- Passport number
- Phone numbers
- Email addresses
- Home address
- User IDs and passwords
- Utility bill account number
- Driver's license number
- Loan account numbers

☐ Insurance account numbers for your health, vehicle, life, etc.

☐ _____

One piece of your data in the hands of a thief is not necessarily harmful. However, when a thief aggregates multiple pieces of your PII, then your identity, credit, and savings are relatively easy to steal. Your strategy is to disrupt the data aggregation efforts by ensuring that you separate the links between your PII whenever possible, thus making you a harder target. By doing so, you keep your data from easily being aggregated. Some data are a matter of public record and difficult to hide, such as your home address and phone number, but there are steps you can take to reduce your exposure. For example, if you run a home business you may consider renting a mailbox at a local retail shipping store and using that address for all business correspondence and contact information on your website. Using this approach, you disassociate your business address from your home address and, thus, reduce your exposure.

A thief may steal your car or break into your home and take your belongings. Your personal space is violated but in both instances; the crime probably ends with that single action. However, your PII is perpetual money in the bank for a predator. When someone steals your PII, this can result in long-term ramifications to your credit, cause you to incur enormous debt, and cause you untold effort and stress as you try to rectify the issues with creditors, banks, and business associates. You must develop a plan that protects your PII to the maximum extent possible. Actions you can take to reduce your exposure are:

☐ Purchase a shredder and use it

☐ Monitor your credit report on a regular basis

☐ Subscribe to a fraud alert service

☐ Password protect your credit cards from unauthorized account charges

☐ Permanently close old credit accounts you no longer use

☐ Insist on making credit card account closures irreversible

☐ Talk with your bank and credit card companies about imposing fraud alert limits on your accounts to ensure you are notified long before an issue becomes a problem

☐ _____

These are all easy steps you can take to reduce your exposure, and many are inexpensive or free. Most lenders, mortgage companies, and credit card companies want to ensure your security for their self-interest. They employ the latest fraud detection tools and will work with you to establish a good security plan or make sure you understand their security procedures to protect your interests. Just as the free market has created a mechanism to target you through advertising, the same market has created a security apparatus that you can use to help protect yourself.

Do Not Share Your PII

You never know who is sharing your information, so it is up to you to be vigilant in your effort to protect your PII. Be cautious with telemarketers and call centers, even from known businesses with whom you deal, because nowadays a lot of this work is outsourced. Whether it is a call center in Des Moines or New Delhi, these call centers do not necessarily have your best interests in mind, or probably even the best interests of the company they represent. They are a clearinghouse for businesses marketing to a broad audience, and they provide cheap, first-tier customer service for goods and services. Often, the call center workers are not employees of the companies they represent but are contractors who perform a particular service for the company.

As a rule, <u>never</u> give out personal information to anyone who calls you. The caller may ask you to verify the information they already have, but legitimate calls from banks and credit card companies do not ask you for your information in this manner. For example, you may receive a call from your credit card company asking you to verify a purchase you made because the purchase tripped a fraud alert their algorithm identified as a distinct departure from your normal purchasing pattern. In this case, the credit card representative does not ask you what purchases you recently made. They give you several choices, one of which is the actual purchase you made, and ask you to verify the legitimate one. **If you receive a call informing you that someone made a suspect purchase using your credit card, and the caller asks you to provide your card number and date of birth as verification of your identity, you can be assured the call is <u>not</u> legitimate.** Do not respond! Hang up immediately and call your bank or credit card company to alert them about the suspicious call you just received. Odds are you are not their only customer receiving such calls. The bottom line is you should never provide your account numbers, Social Security Number, date of birth, or other PII unless you are the one who initiates the call, and you are sure you are talking to a legitimate representative of that business.

Social Engineering and Phishing Schemes

You have probably heard the terms "social engineering" and "phishing." Social engineering involves several independent steps of psychological manipulation to lower your guard and get you to divulge your PII. Phishing is a social engineering technique and, much like fishing in the traditional sense, bait is offered as a deception. The same principles apply across the board, whether it is an unsolicited phone call, email, or text message: if you do not initiate the contact, you should not provide any PII in response. 100 percent of the time, this type of communication is a ploy launched by a predator.

In social engineering scams, the intent is to convince you to take some action that will allow the predator access to your computer, home, bank accounts, etc. For example, you may receive an email from a company that you normally do business with, and the email looks legitimate at first glance. The message may be something routine like a privacy policy update. Many companies send these out regularly. When you open the email, it may ask you to click on a web link to view the new privacy policy. When you click on the link, the program associated with that link downloads malware on your computer that the predator can then use to exploit your computer for passwords, bank account numbers, and other personal information. The link may take you to a blank page or to a site that looks legitimate. Looks do not matter in this case. By going to the link you have opened a path to your computer. Someone has socially manipulated you into doing something you would not otherwise do. With any of these types of social engineering scams, it is important to examine the contents of the email or text before following any link. Though these emails or texts look legitimate, they often are not what they appear. Pay particular attention to the URL address. Because a URL is hard to take over, it will often appear to be something close to a legitimate business when, instead, it is a unique and contrived address. As an example, a valid address may be:

https://online.americanexpress.com

The contrived address by the predator, however, may be:

http://online.americanexpress3681.com or

http://online.americanexpressspecial.com

We are all accustomed to seeing a variety of characters and words in the address line, so at first glance, this may look like it is coming from American Express when in reality you have become a predator's target.

Some very common phishing ploys routinely appear on the Internet in various forms. The gist of the ploy is that an estranged person in Nigeria, Croatia, or some other faraway place has fallen on bad times and has applied for asylum in the United States. Their assets, usually in the millions, cannot be released from a foreign bank without someone stateside vouching for them and receiving the money on their behalf. They ask for your help, maybe because of the type of business you have or your social contacts. They promise you a significant amount of money as compensation for your time and effort in helping them—an offer that can be very enticing if you need the money. The predator usually asks you for your bank account information and other PII so he can wire you the money in advance of your help. Once the predator obtains your bank account information, he can then aggregate it with any other PII he collects about you. At that point, he has enough information to begin exploiting your identity.

Another variation of this scheme is where the predator asks you to wire him money through a wire transfer service such as MoneyGram, Western Union, or even PayPal. He tells you he will use it to pay the "government" fees to get the funds released and give you a percentage of the money released as compensation for your assistance. Whatever the variation, once you provide your bank account information, which "his government requires," or you wire funds to him, then the predator just withdraws or accepts your money, and you never hear from him again.

You may receive an email that appears to come from a family member or close friend. The email may say something like *"I am on vacation in Paris and was robbed last night. They stole everything, cell phone, money, and credit cards. Can you please help me get home? I missed my flight, and I need money to pay for the hotel and get another ticket."* The email will provide a contact where you should wire or PayPal the money so your family member or friend can retrieve it. This type of scam can initially capture your attention because the email address is that of your friend or family member. In these scenarios, the predator puts you in a position where the information cannot be verified. You can't call the hotel; you can't call the person and confirm because they "lost their cell phone" in the robbery; you are left with limited communication options and the urge to help someone you know who is in distress. The email address is, by the way, legitimate.

What has happened is the predator has implanted malware on the person's computer who sent you the story of being robbed. This malware was likely implanted on their computer when the person clicked on an infected link. The malware probably sent the same email to everyone in the person's address book as well. Instead of an email, the predator may take over the person's Facebook, Twitter, or other social media account and send the message from there, making the scam seem all the more legitimate.

In every case these scenarios, or any variation, are a scam—NO EXCEPTIONS!

Medical Data

When you use your rewards card at the drugstore or the supermarket pharmacy, the terms of use generally allow that business to sell your information for marketing purposes. The problem is, the analysis of your prescription drug purchases might provide insights into your medical condition and may fall completely outside of HIPAA laws because the data were not derived from medical records. Some medications have multiple uses, so analytical outcomes could be wrong and, thus, violate your desire for privacy. It's a good idea to avoid using rewards cards or credit cards when you buy sensitive prescription medications, if possible.

Your PII is your most valued asset. With your PII a predator can acquire your money and property. You must make every attempt to prevent aggregation and exploitation of your information by vigilantly monitoring your exposure and footprint in the world.

Account Monitoring and Fraud Protection

Regardless of the effort you expend to secure your PII, your existence in this modern world exposes your private information and financial data every day. Every time you make a purchase with a credit or debit card or pay a utility bill online with your bank routing number and account number, you are giving the predator an opportunity to skim your information. Vigilance and early detection are critical to preventing significant financial loss in cases of identity theft and credit card abuse. A few preventative steps you should take are:

- Self-monitor your financial accounts weekly. Look for anomalies and things out of your regular pattern.
- Place fraud alerts on your credit by contacting the three major credit bureaus:
    - Equifax
    - Experian
    - TransUnion
- Contact your credit card companies and request they put fraud detection alerts on your accounts in the event of significant purchases. That amount should be determined based on your usual credit habits and income.
- Consider employing a fraud detection service like LifeLock, Identity Guard, or TrustediD, which monitor your accounts and activities for signs of fraud and abuse. These companies do not

do much more than what you can do to monitor your accounts and initiate fraud alerts. However, the benefit they offer is the ability to automate the process and do the monitoring for you quickly and efficiently. Also, you do not have to monitor your credit and accounts as frequently. There is the school of thought that suggests by hiring one of these companies to monitor your accounts you make yourself more vulnerable. After all, they now have access to your information which makes you susceptible to insider threat and hacks from that company. The bottom line is that your information is already exposed. Having a monitoring service adds minimal risk and significant gain. Remember, vigilance is the key. No service is perfect, and nothing can detect every possible variation of fraud, but these companies provide a valuable service when coupled with other detection methods.

Insurance

Using the Prevention, Deterrence, and Defense (PDD^{TM}) strategy will reduce your risk, but it won't eliminate it entirely. If you find yourself in the unfortunate situation of having been the target of a predator, then having insurance is critical to limiting the impact.

Renter and homeowner policies cover the household contents, but they typically have coverage limits on high-value items such as electronics, computers, cameras, jewelry, and so forth. Insurance companies offer "Riders" for these items. Like most things you are trying to protect, it is the cost benefit analysis that drives the decision on when and how much to spend on additional coverage. Riders go beyond standard policies to cover those items you feel need coverage or extra coverage. In most cases, Riders are additional affordable coverage on your policy that can provide peace of mind.

There are a variety of insurance offerings for just about anything you can imagine, so consider some of the specialty types that cover beyond the standard automobile, life, renter, and homeowner policies.

Identity theft affects millions of people each year in the United States, and it can be time-consuming and expensive to resolve. Every month or so the news media is covering another company or government agency that has had their customer data stolen. Consider these insights into identity theft:

- The hacker or hacker group who steals the information is looking to make their money in selling the data. Those who buy the data are the ones who use your PII to commit fraud. They use your identity to obtain new credit cards or loans which they use to buy goods and services. Law Enforcement finds this type of crime challenging because it is a significant investment in time and resources to pursue a case.
- Medical records are a prime target for identity thieves.
- Children and the elderly are increasingly targeted by identity thieves because the time from theft to detection is potentially extended over many years.

In many cases, people who fall victim to identity theft discover the crime only after the fact and it is usually at an inconvenient time, such as, when you are applying for credit for something you need (e.g., new car, major house repair, etc.). What are your options?

Many of the major insurance providers are now providing Identity Theft Insurance to their customers. A combination of credit monitoring and Identity Theft Insurance is the best loss mitigation strategy for identity theft. Many employers are now offering Identity Theft Insurance as a benefit option.

Your personal information puts you at risk of identity theft, but your name, job title, profession, where you live, the car you drive, and similar attributes can put you at risk of being targeted for frivolous litigation. The perception that value can be derived by filing a lawsuit against you is a possibility if you have assets to protect. There is also the possibility that someone may feel they have legitimate cause to file a lawsuit against you. In either case, a "Personal Liability" policy is offered by most major insurance carriers and can help protect against a court judgment.

If you have a permit that allows you to carry a concealed weapon legally, then consider maintaining insurance to cover you in a use of force event. Use of force is more of a niche insurance market, but there are insurance carriers who provide this type of coverage, and it is affordable. More so, it can provide other benefits such as a list of attorneys specializing in use of force situations which can be very helpful in extremely stressful circumstances.

As the noted French scientist, Louis Pasteur said, and it applies to all matters relating to personal security awareness, *"chance favors the prepared mind."*

AREA OF VULNERABILITY
Personally Identifiable Information

Use the following checklist to break down the broad area of personally identifiable information into sub-systems or vulnerabilities.

Identify those areas of PII that are vulnerable to attack:
- ☐ Purchase patterns
- ☐ Financial data
- ☐ Medical data
- ☐ _____

Identify those things you are vulnerable to:
- ☐ Telemarketing solicitations
- ☐ Email scams
- ☐ Office theft
- ☐ Data breaches at credit card companies, retailers, hospitals, and others
- ☐ Aggregation of your data
- ☐ _____

PDD™ CHECKLIST
Personally Identifiable Information

Now that you understand some of the vulnerabilities and risk mitigation options regarding personally identifiable information, use the following checklist to begin developing your security posture.

Prevention: What can you do to prevent becoming a target?
- ☐ Shred all paperwork containing PII
- ☐ Subscribe to a fraud alert program
- ☐ Review your credit report every six months
- ☐ Permanently close old credit card accounts you no longer use and make closures irreversible
- ☐ Set fraud alerts on credit card and bank accounts
- ☐ Lock your computer when away
- ☐ Secure all PII at work and school in a locked cabinet or desk
- ☐ Don't use rewards cards or credit cards when purchasing sensitive medications
- ☐ _____

Deterrence: What can you do to deter an attack once you become a target?
- ☐ Do not provide any PII to anyone who calls you; verify only information the caller already has
- ☐ Never open a link sent to you in email or text unless you are sure it is legitimate
- ☐ Never provide PII over an unsecure or non-https:// web address
- ☐ Never send money to any solicitation or warning of inappropriate web searching
- ☐ _____

Defense: What can you do if you are attacked?
- ☐ Report suspicious activity to your fraud alert provider immediately
- ☐ If your credit or debit card has been compromised, ask the provider to close the cards and issue new ones
- ☐ Report evidence of mail fraud to the Postmaster General

☐ Block suspicious/phishing email addresses

☐ Report foreign email scams looking for money or personal information to the FBI

☐ _____

6 COMMUNICATIONS SECURITY: COMPUTERS, PHONES, AND SOCIAL MEDIA

Communications is a complex topic because simply by participating you become vulnerable. The objective here is to help you understand the risks and empower you to make conscious, informed decisions on the actions you take when using various forms of communications. Numerous websites and government forums describe how to manage your privacy features on social networking sites and provide volumes of information on computer and Internet security. However, most of the available information reads like a technical manual and tells you to chase the latest fad in antivirus or encryption software or advises you how to set your privacy settings to protect your stored data. Instead of looking at technical methods to enhance your security, we will take a less complicated view of communications security where we explore it more from a behavioral aspect rather than a technical aspect. No technical tool, whether encryption or antivirus software, can save you from yourself. You must practice security awareness and good behavior for these technical tools to be effective.

Rule Number 1, and actually the only rule, is that there are <u>no</u> take backs, <u>no</u> second chances, and <u>no</u> do-overs where social media and the Internet are concerned. Ever! If you learn nothing else from this chapter, this rule is the most relevant and important. If you end up with a compromised credit card, you simply get a new one. However, if you or someone else posts a picture of you on the Internet, drunk and naked, there are no do-overs. The photo is out there forever for anyone with an interest in you to discover.

Some companies claim they can erase your negative presence and restore your online reputation. Do not believe their claims! They are misleading you to get your money. A company cannot erase or get rid of the negative information that is posted online about you. What the company attempts to do is to bury the negative information in the enormous amount of data on the Internet and make more positive data the first to be found in searches. Negative information never goes away. It never disappears. If you ever put it online, it stays online and creates vulnerabilities for you.

Today's employers use the major search engines to perform background checks before bringing anyone in for a job interview. If you want to know how the world sees you, search your name, profile, and work history before ever applying for a job. Never, ever, let anyone ask you a question about yourself that you do not already know how to answer. This applies to virtually every circumstance in your life. When you go to a job interview, you should always know what everyone else could know about you before you arrive.

Antivirus Software

There are varying opinions on antivirus software. The computer-savvy have their views on which antivirus software is best; nearly all agree that pre-loaded antivirus software that comes with a new machine is not necessarily the best choice, nor is it a good option. If you ask a dozen different Information Technology (IT) experts, you will likely get a dozen different opinions about antivirus software. If you ask a computer sales person in one of the big box stores, they will recommend whatever antivirus software the store is featuring for sale at that time.

Any of the major brand-name, U.S. made, antivirus programs are, under most circumstances, entirely suitable. It is important that you have a current antivirus program installed on your computer and that you keep the updates current. Do not use foreign made antivirus software. They can introduce as many viruses as they prevent. Do not surf the Internet, even once, without an active antivirus program. If your program has expired, then you should connect to the antivirus site and renew your subscription before continuing to use your computer. Otherwise, you fully compromise your PII, whether resident on the computer or accessed through the bank accounts or shopping sites you visit.

However, be aware that antivirus software is just another layer of a multi-layered defense to protect your computer. If you become a target, antivirus software will not be effective against a sophisticated or determined attacker.

Secure Internet Connections

Never give out your PII over an unsecured "http" connection. For example, when you go to an unfamiliar site to shop, check the URL on the address line where you are about to pay. If the address does not start with "https://" then do not trust the site with your PII and credit card information. The "s" at the end of "https" indicates the site is an encrypted and secure data link and is not transmitting your information in the clear or unencrypted.

Software

Before you install any application or software update not proprietary to your operating system manufacturer, you should research the application or update to obtain information about what you are loading. In most cases, your antivirus software manufacturer will have a user forum or Frequently Asked Questions (FAQs) section which can provide helpful information about malware being proliferated at any given time. Often a quick Internet search on the application or update reveals significant information regarding the efficacy of the software in question. Take the time to understand what you are loading or installing. It can save you from having to factory reset your device because of malware or simply poor software code.

Internet Browsing

As you browse the Internet, many websites you visit will download small pieces of information to your computer to aid in advertising or to enhance your user experience. These "cookies", as they are called, may come from the website you visit or from the providers of the advertising banners or other graphics that make up a web page. Surfing a single website can result in the downloading of cookies from several different sources. You may never visit the sites of the major advertisers but still have cookies from those sites downloaded on your computer from surfing the web. Cookies contain a domain where they are valid, an identifier, so the site recognizes them, and usually, a time and date stamp for which the cookies are valid. Cookies allow a site to recognize you on repeat visits, enhancing your user experience and marketing those things that are of particular interest to you. **However, cookies are essentially used to track your Internet patterns, interests, and originating IP address.**

If you do not want to leave a browsing history on your computer, then you need to use the private function in whatever browser you are using. In Internet Explorer, the function is called "InPrivate" and in Google Chrome it is called "incognito." Remember, if your computer is stolen, seized, or manipulated through malware the predator can easily see your habits and interests if you do not use a private browsing feature. However, these in-private browsing features do not hide your Internet surfing habits from your employer if using a work network, your Internet service provider, or the websites you visit. These functions only hide your browsing habits from the exploitation of the computer itself.

For anonymously searching the web, you should use an anonymizer tool like TOR. TOR stands for The Onion Router. TOR obfuscates or hides your originating IP address and disassociates the IP addresses you visit. From their website, the Tor Project is "a US 501(c)(3) non-profit dedicated to the research, development, and education of online anonymity and privacy". TOR is a free download and is regularly maintained with patches and updates. When you use the TOR browser to surf the web, TOR obfuscates your IP address so you cannot be located, and it also prevents cookies and downloads from being loaded onto your computer. However, there is a caveat: you must always use the TOR browser within the defined parameters or you could be compromised without ever knowing. The TOR web page provides instructions and FAQs that explain, in detail, the capabilities and limitations of the system. The TOR system was originally developed by the U.S. Government, much like how the Internet came into existence. The code was released under a free license, and the TOR project itself was established in 2006. Today, the TOR project continues to receive funding from the U.S. government.

Remember, no technical tool or aid is perfect or foolproof. Nothing can save you from bad habits.

There are ongoing efforts worldwide to hack or break TOR to identify a user and a user's location. This activity is, in fact, how the TOR project engineers continue to learn and protect the system. However, like any other technical tool, you must use TOR carefully and within the designed parameters. Similar to a gun, unless you take the time to understand how it works and how you should safely deploy it, you are putting yourself at greater risk.

Remember there are two basic techniques for safe Internet browsing, many tools but two techniques.

1. Use your browser's "private" feature when surfing the web. This action keeps your browsing history and related cookies from being downloaded or stored on your computer. However, this does not hide your originating IP address.

2. Use an anonymizer that obfuscates your originating and ending IP addresses and keeps your browsing history and related cookies from being downloaded or stored on your computer.

Because an anonymizer can be more cumbersome to use than an "in private" search function, and both are more cumbersome than surfing the web in the open, which technique you use should be based on your level of risk and your concern of exploitation.

Embedded Links

Embedded links or URLs are one of the central methods predators use to get malware on your computer or device. Predators bury a virus or rootkit in a hyperlink. When you click on the link, it launches the virus and implants it on your device or computer. Having an up-to-date antivirus software can aid in catching these viruses, but the only way to prevent this kind of attack is to never, ever, click on an embedded link from unsolicited emails. Even following a link sent from a friend can be dangerous if the friend directly forwarded something without due diligence. This action spreads major computer viruses.

Never respond to pop-ups warning of a violation of child porn laws or Internet trafficking. These pop-ups are phishing ploys 100 percent of the time. This Internet scam generally takes on one of two forms. The first type may use intimidation and fear of imprisonment to get you to send money to a "government" office to keep the activity from being reported. The second form may involve burying a virus or implant in the link, which the predator then intends to use to hack your PII. These ploys are a scam 100 percent of the time. Close the window immediately and if the window will not close, which is sometimes the case, restart your computer.

Ransomware

Ransomware is a form of malware that once embedded on your computer or infrastructure allows the predator to confiscate or lock your data, so you no longer have access. Once the predator has control over your data, they will make demands for money in return for giving you back your access. Amazingly, this is becoming a very common form of extortion in spite of the fact that it is so easily prevented.

Ransomware only works if you do not have control of your data. That is why it is so important to back up your data either locally or with one of the cloud providers.

Bad things happen. Whether it is a lightning storm or a digital assault from Eastern Europe, you should back up your data, at the very least, on a daily basis.

Cloud Backup or Local Backup for Your Data

While Google, Apple, Microsoft, and others offer cloud backup services, it is always better to do a local backup of your data. Data you entrust to a storage vendor is something you trust them to secure, so essentially it is compromised. For backing up your computer files and giving you a way to restore all of your information, consider using an external hard drive with backup software and an encryption program. If you use a Mac, OSX will perform encrypted backups without having to load any additional software. You can purchase a backup hard drive for a few hundred dollars and often significantly less, which gives you complete control of your data. It is always a good idea to back up your computer because it will eventually crash. Backup storage of your data ensures you do not lose your valuable data and makes recovery easy and quick in the event of a system failure or if you have to factory reset your device. Because you likely keep sensitive personal data and volumes of interesting pictures on our computer, you should backup your computer, in some fashion, at least daily. Keep the backup drive in a fireproof safe or lock box so you can protect your sensitive data if there is a fire in your home.

However, many people opt for storing and backing up their data on one of the cloud services for fear of losing an external hard drive to theft or fire. These services provide good functionality because they allow you access to your data across all your devices. You can access your data anywhere you have an Internet connection. Cloud storage and backup are convenient and easy, although you are entrusting your data to someone else. A commercial cloud service should not use your information in a nefarious way; however, if someone compromises the cloud infrastructure, then data you store there is compromised. If your cloud storage is hacked, a predator has access to everything you have elected to store. Should you decide to use cloud services for data storage or system backup, consider the following:

- Only put non-sensitive and generic data in the cloud, which includes
  - No PII
  - No compromising pictures, emails, or documents
  - No passwords whatsoever, whether or not encrypted
- Consider using private cloud storage that you can access when you are away from your computer. You can purchase private

cloud storage for a couple of hundred dollars, depending on the amount of storage you want, and it can be set up in your home. The private cloud connects to your secure Wi-Fi and acts like any other cloud storage, but you own it! You save all your data on your computer, which then syncs the data with your cloud storage. You can then access your data from anywhere you have an Internet connection. Private cloud storage is an excellent alternative to public cloud storage and offers you full control of your hardware and encrypted access. The drawback, however, is that the private cloud server has to sit out in your home connected to the Internet to work, which means it is not without risk as a system backup because it could be stolen from your home or consumed in a fire. If you use a private cloud, you should still maintain an external hard drive for system backup that you keep locked up in a safe place.

Wi-Fi Connectivity

Lock it down, period! If you have an open Wi-Fi network, you are not vulnerable—you are compromised! You must protect your Wi-Fi with a strong password. If all of your teenager's friends know your Wi-Fi password, then it is no longer secure. If you have teenage children or a lot of guests using your Wi-Fi, consider having two routers—your "guest" access point and your secure home access point. Some routers have the inherent ability to create two networks and can provide a home network and a separate guest network in one box. A minimal investment can save you thousands of dollars in damages.

Do not ever use public, unsecured, non-password-protected networks, like those that you find at the airport or the local coffee shop, for any online activity in which you give out PII such as credit card numbers, tax information, birth date, or checking account information. In fact, as a rule, it is better to stay completely off public Wi-Fi networks at hotels and restaurants/fast food joints, regardless of whether they are password protected. The passwords are so proliferated in some public environments they are easy prey for a predator. Once on the network, the predator can then exploit the other users. If you travel a lot, consider employing a personal Wi-Fi hotspot or a smartphone-based hotspot, which allows you to carry a private, secure network with you wherever you go.

Passwords

Having "strong" passwords and changing them often are critical defensive measures that will keep your accounts safe from hackers. Passwords can be challenging: if you make them secure, you likely will not remember them! Like everything else, there are tradeoffs, and you have to find the balance between a strong password and something you can remember. You can have a strong password randomly generated using a number of available online programs, or you can make one yourself following these rules:

- Minimum 16 characters
- Minimum 3 upper- and 3 lower-case letters
- Minimum 3 special characters and three numbers
- No more than 3 of the same character in a row

There are many schools of thought about passwords and their complexity. Using the rules above, you may end up with a password like d#Gh@UR*S2P6zbS%. This may be a strong password, but if you have 20 different passwords like this one you will never remember any of them. The use of a good password manager can significantly help in freeing up your mind from trying to remember complex passwords and by providing another hardened security layer to your defensive posture. There are many good password managers available online. Research the capabilities and reviews before purchasing one. Though efficient in the long run, password managers can be cumbersome on initial set up.

The truth is, it is very difficult to break a password using brute force computing. In most cases, the hacker does not "break" your password. The hacker exploits code flaws in a program or a service provider to identify your password or bypass it. The other common technique for gaining access to your accounts is the use of phishing ploys. This occurs when you click on an embedded email link and launch an implant that exploits your computer and allows the hacker to identify or bypass your passwords. It is critical that you never:

- Reuse passwords, or
- Use the same passwords across multiple accounts. If a predator exploits one of your accounts, then you must make it an equal amount of work for him to hack another account.

To find the right balance between security, reality, and something that works for you, you might choose passwords that are not as complicated as the randomly generated ones described previously but are still secure. As a suggestion, the following guidelines will yield a secure password but will provide you with something more easily remembered:

- Minimum 8 characters
- Made of 2 unrelated words that are a minimum of 4 letters each (you can find a number of random word generators on the Internet) Ensure you do not use words that have any special meaning in your life: wife's name, college mascot, your street name, etc.

- Minimum 2 uppercase letters
- Minimum 2 numbers or 2 special characters
- Change your passwords every 90 days

Examples:

RoofWing00

BadgerBloat66

@BecauseFormalRebel1

The more random words you use, the more secure the password. To help remember your passwords, think of them as phrases.

Cell Phones and Computers

Your cell phone and computer carry so much of your life that to lose them or have them compromised exposes you to risks you never before imagined. It is important to understand, at least at a rudimentary level, how others can track your phone and computer and exploit you. The computer and phone have different issues about which you need to be aware.

From the first day your phone is turned on and set up for you in the store, it is forever identified with you and your account. Every time you turn on your phone, the first thing that happens is the phone reaches out and contacts the nearest cell tower. The phone is then registered on the network. This action allows you to make a phone call. Each cell tower has a unique identifier and is geo-located in a variety of public and private databases. Once your phone identifies with a tower, which takes only seconds, you can be located to within a mile or so without ever making a phone call or sending a text. Your phone registers with the cell network whether it has a SIM card or its Location Services are turned on. However, it is currently NOT possible to locate your phone to the exact latitude and longitude when Location Services are turned off. This is one of a number of reasons why you should keep Location Services turned off at all times, except when you need the GPS for navigation. In that case, turn on Location Services only for the period of time you are using Maps and then turn Location Services off again.

Keeping Location Services off significantly increases the effort it takes to track and locate the exact position of your phone. The disadvantage with keeping Location Services off is that if your phone is lost or stolen some recovery apps will not allow you to turn the GPS on remotely. Thus, you no longer have your phone's location. However, you can still remotely reset the phone and delete all of your data.

On most modern phones, turning on Location Services turns on the GPS, but it also allows the phone to use nearby cell tower IDs and Wi-Fi network IP addresses to identify your location in rapid fashion. This is a convenience for you in that your map services operate at lightning speed. The disadvantage is that your phone has been identified, not just with a GPS location, but with specific cell towers and IP addresses. Over time, collection software or malware can use this information to identify specific patterns and vulnerabilities in your life. A predator can use this information to target you, your resources, and family when they know you are out of pattern.

Remember, the only way your phone cannot be exploited is when it is turned off. When you turn off your phone, it will know, either by cell tower or GPS, where it was turned off. The network will also know, and that information will be associated with you and your account. When you turn on the phone it, and the network will register where it was turned on. **However, neither the phone nor the network will register where the phone has been while it was off.** On many modern phones, you cannot remove the phone's battery. However, if you can remove the battery, you add an additional obstacle to the predator because the carrier, or a representative of the carrier, can manipulate your phone with the battery installed, whether the phone is on or off.

To minimize your risks, do not use your work computer or company-supplied cell phone for ANY personal business. What you do on company time and company-supplied systems leaves a permanent record. The law requires most businesses to have a data retention policy. Today many of those companies either reserve the right or execute their right to monitor your activities when you use company resources. Most large companies will actively monitor their computers and phones. Often this is under the guise of security against insider threat. Consequently, they monitor any personal activity on those devices, such as your search habits, email, and contacts. There is little latitude here. If you have a company or government supplied device, do not ever use it for personal activities. Should you choose to accept that risk, then your only risk mitigation is to be extremely cautious about what websites you visit, what you put in personal emails, and what you choose to store or download on the company-supplied devices you have. This is onerous.

Using Your Own Device at Work

The workplace holds unique risks. Because of the spread of violence in the workplace and the proliferation of the Internet and social media, many companies have implemented comprehensive monitoring of their employees. In many cases, these actions help to ensure an employee's safety, in other circumstances they can be personally invasive. As the technical world continues to evolve, more companies are moving to the "Bring Your Own Device" (BYOD) model where a company installs their email client on YOUR device so you can send and receive work emails. There are pros and cons to this model from a privacy perspective. BYOD is convenient for you because you can use your own device for both personal and professional business. Also, BYOD significantly reduces company costs incurred when purchasing devices and airtime. The email client typically runs as a system app and collects a lot of information about your device such as location, IP address, and contacts.

Now, the real question is how much of your data does the company collect and store from your personal device? When your company loads the email client on your device, it also loads various security packages to protect their program and their data and to monitor the program's diagnostics. With some knowledge of the current state of technology and with some technical information about the email program your company uses, you could find out what they collect and how often. However, without that level of specificity and constant monitoring to see when the program changes, it is impossible for you to determine what your real threat is from an employer who is monitoring your activities. Remember that laptops and cell phones have microphones and cameras, so the risk goes well beyond having access to your emails, location data, and contacts.

There are ways to mitigate the risk to you and your personal data so that you do not need to "geek out" about what has been loaded on your device. If you BYOD, whether it is a smartphone, tablet, or computer, know and fully understand your company's policies on employee monitoring. The company must disclose its policies. Get a copy of this policy at least once a year to identify any changes the company makes as technology evolves. You will likely be surprised at how aggressive many companies are with their IT policies.

Be aware that once you allow someone to load a program on your phone, your phone is then compromised. This is not to say you should not BYOD. After all, it is easy and very convenient for you. Just be aware of the consequences as you conduct your personal and professional business.

Anything that the company's program collects from your phone becomes a part of the company's permanent record and, consequently, can be accessed by insider threat and government enforcement. ALL email clients collect and store the IP address where you access the Internet. There are publicly available databases that identify the location of virtually every IP address in the United States. Though the locational data does not resolve to a latitude and longitude, it will define the specific neighborhood or part of the city where an IP address is located. Consequently, your location is always known within a few miles. The only way to prevent being located by where you access the Internet is to use an anonymizer and most companies will not allow their email client to run through an anonymizer. If you feel you are allowing access to more information than you are comfortable with, simply factory reset your device. You are under no obligation, by most employers, to bring your own device. This convenience merely allows companies to save money on hardware and you to carry one device instead of two.

Always be vigilant and keep your devices free of compromising information and pictures. You should be extra cautious if you load a company program on your personal device. The naked picture that seemed like a good idea at midnight can be exploited. The IP addresses of the headhunters you have been visiting online can be exploited. Any especially sensitive information should not be stored on a device or accessed through a device that has a company program installed.

Work Conduct

Be mindful of exposing too much of your PII to coworkers. Just because you are all in a close and trusted environment does not mean everyone is honest. That is why you should always lock up your purse or handbag in a desk or locker. Lock your computer whenever you are not close by, and never share passwords with co-workers. Once someone has access to your computer or account, they can cause a great deal of damage within minutes.

If you receive inappropriate text messages or emails, do not respond. Inappropriate means telling an off-color joke or spreading office rumor and innuendo. If you and a friend want to discuss what the boss is doing with a client, or why Joe got promoted instead of Jane, have this conversation in person or on your private phones. It is important to stay above office politics and not to write down anything you would not say to your friends or your boss. Remember, you never know with any degree of certainty whether your conversations are being recorded. Consider, for instance, that the state of Virginia is a one-party state. As long as you are involved in the conversation, it is legal for you to record it without the other party's permission.

Precautions With Your Devices

Consider the use of a password-protection application. There are many available password-protection apps which will encrypt all your different passwords in a single location. These apps allow you to unlock the file with a single password. Some of these apps are good, but some have backdoors that a predator can exploit. Using any of them is better than storing your passwords openly on your phone or computer. Keep in mind; everything is exploitable over time. If you choose to use one of these applications, make sure you change the primary application password regularly—every 30 days is not too often, considering that connected to this one password are all the passwords to everything else in your life.

Do not use apps that come from non-U.S. software manufacturers for any PII, backup, or passwords. Many of these foreign-developed applications contain backdoors and malware. Often these applications extract your contacts and locational data and send it to a foreign-based server. Protection of data is rare in these circumstances and increases your overall exposure exponentially.

You should conduct an online search of hacker reviews for any encryption application or storage service you are considering. There are communities of coders who hack on programs and code to find their vulnerabilities and backdoors. These hackers attempt to break into programs, applications, and networks just to find their weaknesses and then post them online. This hacking activity goes on 24 hours a day, every day, and it is very difficult to compete with this kind of crowd-sourced information. This is the central tenant behind the concept of safety through awareness, not technology. Use the information publicly available to inform you and help you take advantage of your position.

Lock your cell phone with a random PIN and change the PIN every 90 days. Remember, make yourself a hard target. Not using a PIN to lock your cell phone or using a standard factory pin, such as 0000 or 1234, makes you a very easy target. In the best-case scenario, someone steals your cell phone, resets it, and has a free phone. In the worst-case scenario, the thief takes your cell phone, retrieves your passwords and PII off the phone, and exploits your PII. Consider enabling the setting that will completely erase the data from your device after ten unsuccessful PIN attempts.

Be Aware of Digital Association

The principle reason that everything is associated these days is so someone can exploit your in-pattern life for marketing purposes. However, the collateral risk in having these associations is that one misplaced phone call or text message from your personal or business number forever ties that phone to your life and that of your family. Most employers have a policy that any provided device, whether a cell phone or a computer, is subject to monitoring. It is always best to have a public cell phone, work or otherwise, and a private cell phone that is not connected to your contacts outside of your family. In fact, for your "private" out-of-pattern cell phone it is best to use a prepaid SIM card that you purchase with cash. This makes tracing the phone to you or your contacts very difficult for anyone targeting you.

The key is to maintain an air gap between your patterns of life. This fact holds true, especially for public figures. If you are a public figure and potential target for thieves or terrorists, you should have a work phone provided by, and monitored by, your company or government agency. You should use this phone for your daily business. In addition, maintain a separate cell phone that you have purchased with cash as a prepaid device. Use this phone to call your wife or husband and children. You should also use this phone for personal business like doing mobile banking or buying sports tickets. This method of using separate phones keeps all of your personal and very exploitable information from mixing with your more overt life and all the data of your business persona.

You should never "loan" your cell phone to a stranger or even a casual friend. If someone wants to borrow your cell phone because of an "emergency", do not give it up. Instead, offer to make the call to the police or appropriate authorities for them. If they insist on making the call, then you should be suspicious and refuse to allow them to use your cell phone.

Install a cell phone tracking app on your phone. Most cell phone platforms (e.g., Android, iPhone) have system applications that work with the location software to geo-locate your cell phone in an emergency. Use of these apps can be beneficial in the recovery of your device if lost or stolen and can provide the additional capability of being able to reset your phone remotely and erase your data.

In the event your personal cell phone or device is compromised through malware you should do a factory reset of the device and "start over". This is one reason why it is important to have all your devices properly backed up. If the device is compromised, then you can be back in business with a simple factory reset. Additionally, you should always factory reset your device before disposal.

Social Media Behavior

When it comes to social media behavior, volumes have been written on proper conduct yet so many people still ignore the basic rules. How you conduct yourself on social media will forever follow you throughout your life. Most employers now search potential job applicants' social media activity as part of their hiring and screening process and background check. A social media search can often provide more insight into a person's character, behaviors, and history than traditional background checks did in the past. This fact cannot be overstated: you should always be aware of the risks you assume with your social media activities. The world is different now than it was 30 years ago. This world is not a nicer place, nor is it a safer place because of the Internet. It is a more dangerous and less forgiving world than at any time in history. The social media scene offers enormous opportunity for crowd-sourced violence, aggression, and thievery.

Your online persona is an extension of your reputation. It is your responsibility to manage it and protect it. If you want to have a reputation for honesty, integrity, and high ethical standards, then you must put forth the effort to project such an image online. This includes not posting negative comments about others, addressing issues and not personalities, and reading and re-reading everything you post before you hit the send button. You should always observe the RWE or Red Wine Effect—once you start drinking, you should put down the phone and not post or send emails until the next morning. In the light of day, it is frequently apparent what could have been a bad idea.

Consider the fact that Facebook has a feature that allows friends to "tag" you in a photo when they post. By "tagging" you, what they are doing is enabling Facebook to identify you across multiple accounts and associate you with people and activities. The only control you have over this is to be cautious about where and when you have your picture taken.

Social media scraping is a technique used by marketers, predators, and law enforcement to collect and aggregate data that you publicly expose when you use social media. A variety of tools are available, both open source and proprietary, to perform data collection based on location, subject, user, or any variety of other criteria. The tools work by reaching out on the Internet to collect targeted data based on unique search criteria. They can aggregate any related topics in the public space across multiple sources. For example, using these collection tools, a predator can enter your real name into the system and the tools will begin to scour the Internet, identify, collect, recognize, and collate related data. The entire process only takes a few minutes compared with the methods used before the arrival of social media. Armed with a single piece of information, including your Twitter handle, your Facebook name, or maybe a LinkedIn account name, the predator can get all the information you have publicly posted. This includes your location when you post with Location Services turned on, the text of all your posts, and all associated media. The only way to deter this activity is to lock down your privacy settings on each of the sites you use. However, the information you post is still collected by the host site, just not necessarily released. Your posts are only one change of privacy policy away from being exposed. The dangers associated with using social media are immense. All Tweets about your classmate or co-worker, or threats you post against others, are recorded and publicly available even if they are peer to peer posts. Even when you lock down your privacy settings, this information is only a subpoena or a hack away from being public.

You may choose to have an anonymous account on Instagram, Reddit, or one of the other social media sites or "secure" communications applications. With an anonymous account, you feel you can post your comments and pictures with impunity. You may have an anonymous account on Snapchat where you seek a partner for an affair. Many sites provide encrypted communications, but few sites promote real anonymity. The site or application may not ask you to verify an email address or phone number; you may be able to sign up with a fake name and password and nothing more. However, when you opt into many of these apps, they request or require access to your contacts and phone information. Once you allow access to your contacts and phone ID information, it becomes public record and can be exploited by the developer of the app, predators, or law enforcement. It is imperative to have an air gap between your in-pattern life and your out-of-pattern life.

If you choose to communicate actually "in private," you must use a clean phone or computer that does not have your contacts stored, is not associated with a cell phone account in your name, and from which you do not access your Google, Microsoft, or other web-based accounts. NO EXCEPTIONS!

Before you post anything using your overt, in pattern, cell phone or computer consider whether it is something you would want to see in the local paper or have exposed to the public.

Privacy Policies

Do you actually read the privacy policy when you download a new app or sign up for a new online service? These policies are usually pages of legalese that are unintelligible. You need to realize what you are giving away by agreeing to use the app or the service. Think about what you expose before agreeing to use them. What is almost universally accepted is if you willingly share something, it is considered public information by all social networking sites. Capitalism and marketing primarily drive this, but the side effect is complete transparency. Below are sections from the Facebook Privacy Policy, the Netflix policy, and Verizon's policy. Again, these sections illustrate what you are freely giving away.

From Facebook - <u>*https://www.facebook.com/about/privacy/your-info*</u> *as of December 2014.*

Your information
Your information is the information that's required when you sign up for the site, as well as the information you choose to share.

Public information

When we use the phrase "public information" (which we sometimes refer to as "Everyone information"), we mean the information you choose to make public, as well as information that is always publicly available.

We store data for as long as it is necessary to provide products and services to you and others, including those described above. Typically, information associated with your account will be kept until your account is deleted. For certain categories of data, we may also tell you about specific data retention practices.

We may enable access to public information that has been shared through our services.

We may allow service providers to access information so they can help us provide services.

Cookies
Cookies are small pieces of data that are stored on your computer, mobile phone, or other device. Pixels are small blocks of code on webpages that do things like allow another server to measure viewing of a webpage and often are used in connection with cookies.

Cookies and things like local storage help make Facebook work, like allowing pages to load faster because certain content is stored on your browser or by helping us authenticate you to deliver personalized content.

To learn more about how advertisers generally use cookies and the choices advertisers provide, visit the Network Advertising Initiative, the Digital Advertising Alliance, the Internet Advertising Bureau (US), or the Internet Advertising Bureau (EU).

Refer to your browser or device's help material to learn what controls you can often use to remove or block cookies or other similar technologies or block or remove other data stored on your computer or device (such as by using the various settings in your browser). If you do this, it may affect your ability to use Facebook or other websites and apps.

From Netflix https://www.netflix.com/PrivacyPolicy as of December 2014
- *Information we collect automatically: We collect information regarding you and your interactions with us and our advertising, your use of our service, applications, sites, tools, and customer service, as well as information regarding your computer or other device used to access our service (such as gaming systems, smart TVs, mobile devices, and set top boxes). This information may include:*
  - *your activity on the Netflix service, such as title selections, watch history, and search queries;*
  - *details regarding your interactions with customer service, such as the date, time, and reason for contacting us, transcripts of any chat conversations, and if you call us, your phone number;*
  - *device IDs or unique identifiers, device and software characteristics (such as type and configuration), connection information, statistics on page views, referral URLs, ad data, IP address and standard web log information;*
  - *Information collected via the use of cookies, web beacons and other technologies. See our Cookies and Internet Advertising section for more details.*

From Verizon FiOS privacy policy Information Collected When You Use Verizon Products and Services: We collect information about your use of our products, services, and sites. Information such as call records, websites visited, wireless location, application and feature usage,
network traffic data, product and device-specific information and identifiers, service options you choose, mobile and device numbers, video streaming and video packages and usage, movie rental and purchase data, FiOS TV viewership, and other similar information may be used for billing purposes, to deliver and maintain products and services, or to help you with service-related issues or questions. In addition, this information may be used for purposes such as providing you with information about product or service enhancements, determining your eligibility for new products and services, and marketing to you. This information may also be used to manage and protect our networks, services and users from fraudulent, abusive, or unlawful uses; and help us improve our services, research and develop new products, and offer promotions and other services.

As you can see, you are not just renting a movie or sharing your dinner menu with friends. Everything you post, everything you do online through any of the many apps and programs you use every day simply contributes to the collection of information that is now public and defines you whether you like the definition or not.

These are examples of privacy policies, as of the writing of this book, and are not meant to be authoritative or up-to-date. The point in providing these policy sections is to illustrate that you need to review the privacy policies of those services you use and to understand what you are sacrificing when you agree to their terms and conditions. You must occasionally review the privacy policies because they change often depending on the service provider. You can quickly research a company's privacy policy online.

AREA OF VULNERABILITY
Communications Security
Computers, Phones, and Social Media

Use the following checklist to break down the broad area of communications security into sub-systems or vulnerabilities.

Identify those things that are vulnerable to attack:
- ☐ Computers and phones
- ☐ Unsecure Internet connections
- ☐ Cloud data storage
- ☐ Passwords
- ☐ Company-supplied phones and computers, BYOD apps
- ☐ Professional networking sites
- ☐ Personally Identifiable Information
- ☐ Online posts
- ☐ Internet surfing habits
- ☐ _____

Identify those things that you are vulnerable to:
- ☐ Computer viruses
- ☐ Unsecure websites
- ☐ Software installs
- ☐ Cookies/Browser habits
- ☐ Cell phone applications
- ☐ Social media exploitation
- ☐ Selling of personal data
- ☐ Identity theft
- ☐ Financial fraud
- ☐ Cyberbullying
- ☐ _____

PDD™ CHECKLIST
Communications Security
Computers, Phones, and Social Media

Now that you understand some of the vulnerabilities and risk mitigation options regarding communications security, use the following checklist to begin developing your security posture.

Prevention: What can you do to prevent becoming a target?

- ☐ Install antivirus software on all your devices
- ☐ Use only secure https:// addresses when you send PII or shop online
- ☐ Research apps and software updates before installing
- ☐ Use a private browsing feature when surfing the Internet
- ☐ Never click on links from unknown or suspect addresses
- ☐ Never respond to "government warnings" of illicit behavior
- ☐ Back up your computer data
- ☐ Keep all PII out of the cloud
- ☐ Use only secure Wi-Fi networks
- ☐ Ensure home Wi-Fi is password protected
- ☐ Use strong passwords and change your passwords every 90 days
- ☐ Use a different password for every account
- ☐ Maintain a private cell phone and email account; don't conduct personal business on work-supplied cell phones or computers
- ☐ Understand your company's BYOD policies
- ☐ Do not loan your computer or phone to friends or acquaintances
- ☐ Be cautious about content you post online; think twice before hitting send; keep emails professional and void of rumor, innuendo, and defamation
- ☐ Use a fraud protection service
- ☐ _____

Deterrence: What can you do to deter an attack once you become a target?

- ☐ Monitor your online presence, bank accounts, and utilities for unusual activity at least monthly
- ☐ Report suspicious account activity immediately to the service provider
- ☐ Change passwords immediately upon discovery of suspicious activity

☐ Dispose of private phone numbers and email addresses upon discovery of suspicious activity (hacking)

☐ Change your Wi-Fi network password if you feel you have been compromised

☐ _____

Defense: What can you do if you are attacked?

☐ Have a tracking and self-destruct app on your cell phone and laptop

☐ Factory reset and properly dispose of old hardware, computers, and phones

☐ _____

7 SELF-DEFENSE

"Never walk away from home ahead of your axe and sword.
You can't feel a battle in your bones or foresee a fight."
– The Havamal, circa 1000 AD

As we address the concepts ubiquitous across various aspects of life, let us explore basic self-defense—always a hot and contested topic! Like an IT specialist on antivirus software, every expert in self-defense has an opinion on the best techniques and tools to use for self-protection. Here's the truth: the only effective tools or weapons are those that are handy in an emergency, and the only effective techniques are those that are instinctual. Complex martial arts moves are for the professional. Guns are most often for those who are experienced users. Practically speaking, there are only two phases to self-defense:

1. Avoidance, and

2. Swift, violent action

Avoid Altercations

The best way to survive an altercation is to avoid it! Your first objective should always be to avoid attack altogether. Be conscious of where you travel, what time of the day or night you travel, how you dress, what you post on social media, and how much you drink, among other things. Avoidance is what we do in the prevention and deterrence phases of awareness and safety. However, there may be a time when you cannot avoid an altercation, and that is when you must be prepared to fight.

Swift, Violent Action

Self-defense is the last bastion of survival. No matter who you are or what condition you are in, you should take a self-defense course. Many martial arts studios and some local governments offer pure self-defense classes. They are usually a few hours to a whole day in length. These courses focus on violent self-defense actions that help you subdue or escape an attacker, and they often employ some of the improvised weapons we will talk about later in this chapter. You should attend one of these courses at least annually just to refresh your memory of the techniques. These courses are not for sport and are not artistic martial arts. They provide you with simple, violent defensive techniques that can quickly become intuitive.

In self-defense, your one objective is to disable the threat as quickly as possible and then to get away. The objective is <u>never</u> to stand and fight. You should inflict maximum pain as quickly as possible to disable and distract your attacker (remember the porcupine!) and then remove yourself from the hostile environment. This is called "getting off the X." The X is the place where the attack occurs. Think of it as X marks the spot. The longer you remain on the X, the longer you remain vulnerable. However, it is important to continue to engage until the threat ceases or you can get away. Remember, once you commit to fighting, you must commit 100 percent to swift, violent action.

What can you use to attack your attacker? Where do you attack?

Absent of any additional training, when you have to defend yourself use whatever you have available—pen, keys, stapler, stick, fork, knife, broom handle, glass from a broken bottle or cup—to strike at the assailant.

It boils down to two basic principles.

1. With hard objects and club-like weapons attack joints and bone.

2. With sharp or pointed weapons attack soft tissue.

Targets for club-like weapons include:

- Knees
- Elbows
- Collar bone
- Shins
- Ankles
- Top of the feet
- Genitals – A good target for any weapon

Soft tissue targets include:

- Eyes
- Throat
- Ears
- Kidneys
- Lower Abdomen and Genitals (Male or female it is all painful!)

When an attacker forces you to violence, you must be **relentless, crazed, and committed** until the attacker is subdued and you can get off the X. If an attacker physically assaults you, being nice and considerate is not an option. You are still a victim until you commit to hurt the predator to affect your survival.

Pepper Spray

Although not lethal, pepper spray can be a very effective tool for self-defense. It is a great distraction. Pepper spray does not always stop an assailant cold, a fact that concerns many people. However, that is not the objective when you carry and use pepper spray. For the average person, the purpose of using pepper spray is to buy those precious seconds necessary to get off the X or to inflict maximum pain and physical harm to the assailant. Just as the police use pepper spray to gain an advantage over a perpetrator, the average person should use it for the same purpose. Like a gun, pepper spray is only useful if it is available at a moment's notice. If it is stuffed in the bottom of your purse or backpack or your motorcycle saddlebag, it is not handy. Be diligent; this is what helps you survive an attack. Carry it and have it available.

The "20-foot rule" generally applies regardless of the weapon. The 20-foot rule represents that distance at which we begin to feel threatened and identify a need for action. To understand how important it is to be aware and prepared, have a friend stand 20 feet away from you. Knowing they are there but not knowing when they will attack, have your friend move toward you as if they are attacking you. In 20 feet, you have little time to react. See how quickly you can respond with the pepper spray in your pocket or purse, or in your hand. (It is best, though, not to actually spray your friend in the face.) You will lose every time if you are not aware of the developing threat and prepared for an immediate defense.

Several manufacturers of pepper spray make different form factors to suit your comfort level. A modern form is a two-shot canister shaped like a small pistol for those comfortable with a gun. One of the most commonly used forms is the pressurized spray canister that attaches to a key ring. If you are going to carry pepper spray, attach it to your keys, belt, or pocket. When in higher-threat areas, such as walking to your car at night in the mall parking lot, make sure to carry it in your hand, ready to deploy. An assailant can be on top of you before you have even identified a threat. Predators frequently work in small teams. Disrupting an attack and quickly removing yourself from the situation is your best defense.

Wasp Spray

In an emergency, or if you live in an area where pepper spray is illegal, another great self-defense tool is wasp spray. A full-size can of wasp spray by the front door, in the car, or on the nightstand can be an effective distractor. Roach spray and hairspray work as well, but most wasp sprays produce a stream up to 12 feet, eliminating your need to be close to the attacker. Remember, using wasp, hair, or pepper spray is a strategy you can employ to escape or attack a threat. These sprays do not give you stand-and-fight capability; they allow you a momentary distraction to escape or a split second advantage to attack.

Readily Available Improvised Weapons

After reading through this section, you should look around your house, work, car, purse, or briefcase for all those common everyday items that can be used as a weapon in an emergency. You will be surprised at the self-defense tools that are readily available in your daily life. You are looking for sharp pointed things and club like weapons.

Writing Pen

With a sturdy metal writing pen, you can inflict significant injury. Use the pen as a stabbing device in case of attack. Several weapon manufacturers make solid steel devices that resemble a pen or in some cases even function as a pen but are a solid piece of steel. This type of machined pen is, of course, an effective weapon but it looks like a weapon, and in some cases can be illegal to carry. Many people have been killed in prison by nothing more than a shank. For any stabbing device, you should target your attacker's soft tissue.

Key Ring

If you are like most people, you have a key ring with keys to everything you own. Your key ring is a good emergency weapon. It is best to have a small 4-inch wood or metal rod attached to the key ring to use as a handle. In an attack, grasp the handle and strike at the attacker with the keys. Your keys, used in conjunction with pepper spray, become an effective defensive weapon. You should target your attacker's face and eyes.

Scissors

The perfect shank, scissors can be found at home, work, and often in one's purse or briefcase. They can be used as a stabbing device when closed and as a cutting instrument when open like a straight razor. Any sharp instrument like a knife, razor, scissors, etc., guarantees you are going to inflict significant pain and damage if you aggressively defend yourself against an attacker.

Other Improvised Weapons – What Can You Add?

Your life contains a variety of items you can use as weapons.

- ☐ Golf clubs
- ☐ Baseball bat
- ☐ Kitchen knives
- ☐ Lampstand
- ☐ Frying pan – can be used as a club or a shield against knife attacks
- ☐ Cane
- ☐ Briefcase or purse
- ☐ Nail file

☐ Spiked heel on high heel shoes

☐ _____

Deception as a Defense

To prevent becoming a target you can use deception as a means to appear stronger or more secure than you are. There are hundreds of ways to present a position of strength. The following are examples intended to provoke thought about what may be useful in your life. Develop your deception techniques specific to your environment.

- If you do not have a dog, buy a big bone, a few dog toys, and any other items that make it look like you have a dog. Leave them where a potential thief can see them. Put up a beware of dog sign at your house or apartment, or maybe an "I love my Doberman sticker" on your car.

- Post an NRA sticker, or an "I SUPPORT THE "LOCAL" MARTIAL ARTS STUDIO" bumper sticker on your vehicle.

- Place a sign from a local alarm company in your yard or window even if you cannot afford the alarm system.

- If you cannot afford a home surveillance system, buy one of the fake cameras with the flashing light and place it conspicuously outside your home along with a sign that indicates your property is under video surveillance. Make sure you mount it in an area where it can be seen but not scrutinized, so it 's hard for a predator to determine it is fake.

- _____

Detecting a Stalker

How do you determine if you are being stalked or surveilled? There are complex concepts associated with drawing out and identifying those who may be tracking or following you to gain information about your habits and patterns of life. However, the basic principles that lead to the identification of those targeting you are simple.

Be aware of your surroundings/Look for the unusual

Whether you are a government worker, a bank manager, or a counter clerk at a jewelry store, you have information and access that predators want. Vigilance is the key, and there is a difference between vigilance and paranoia. Vigilant observation will allow you to pick out the anomalies in your life with little disruption; in contrast, paranoia is crippling and does nothing to enhance your state of awareness or security.

Look for unusual behavior. Except for trained professionals, it is very hard for most people to blend into an environment naturally while doing something as unnatural as following you or collecting information about your patterns. Once a predator begins to target you, he begins to expose himself. As part of your everyday life, you should take the time to look at people's habits and behavior. Once you become aware of your normal surroundings, then you can begin to discern out-of-the-norm activities. This is a learned skill. Most people are so self-absorbed in their daily lives and relationships that they do not focus on the complicated world that is developing and changing around them.

To practice this skill, go to the mall, walk around, window shop, and watch the people around you. What are they doing? How do they conduct themselves with friends? Who appears to be alone and seems out of place or to have no purpose? Get used to seeing what's going on in your environment. In time, you will begin to see that the world has its own natural pattern. At that point, you will begin to see those people who do not fit into the typical pattern or rhythm of their surroundings. They will stand out to you as a black and white character in a technicolor movie.

Identify the threat quickly

When you are out and about in your car, on the street, or even in the mall, you are exposed and vulnerable. If you become a target or are being watched or stalked, the sooner you identify this fact, the sooner you can take corrective action. It is like cancer: the earlier you detect it, the greater the likelihood of survival. Similarly, the longer someone is allowed to watch you and your habits, the more information they gain and the more vulnerable you become.

How do you begin to identify a threat? Start by taking note of recurring sightings of the same car or person over time and distance. If you see someone that seems out of place or appears to pop up repeatedly, you must begin to take a defensive posture.

Once an unusual behavior has caught your attention, the next step is to determine whether it is unusual behavior because you are being targeted or whether it is simply unusual behavior exhibited by people on a random basis. When you start paying attention to your surroundings, you will discover a lot of random craziness in the world unrelated to anything nefarious. To make this determination, you want to force the predator to show up repeatedly over time and in multiple, disparate locations. If you identify unusual behavior that occurs in two separate locations over a period of time, the probability is high that you are a target.

For example, if you are out on Saturday morning running errands with a minivan full of kids, you may stop at the local coffee shop for treats all around. It may be a place you frequent, or it may be a place that is simply convenient in your travels. While you are in the coffee shop, you see someone that is out of place. They may stare at you to the point you feel uncomfortable, or they may approach you or try to play with the children. They may ask how you like the coffee or if you live close. People are odd; people are friendly, but if something feels off you should begin to focus your attention. When you leave the coffee shop, watch and see who leaves immediately after you. Did the person that seemed out of place follow you? Are they standing in the window watching to see where you go? It could be coincidental that the person of interest leaves when you leave but at that point, you should be on full alert. Once you get everyone in the minivan, lock the doors and continue on your errands. Focus on your surroundings and changes in those surroundings. Keep to your routine and schedule. Your next stop may be at the post office a half mile away. You should be looking for the person of concern from the coffee shop. Observe whether they are following you or suddenly appear at the post office. Next, you may go to the dry cleaners in the local strip mall down the street from the post office to drop off laundry. Do you see the same person of concern from the coffee shop? Ask yourself if these are places anyone else would be visiting on your exact schedule? Sometimes it is hard to make this determination, especially in a city where coincidental occurrences happen. However, after two encounters with a person of concern over the course of a single day, you should then aggressively seek to expose your predator as quickly as possible.

Draw out your predator

To identify threats as they are developing, you want to put the predator in a position where he has to expose himself. When a predator is hunting, the objective is to stay concealed until time to attack. You want to create an atmosphere where the predator has no cover or place to hide. However, you do not want to confront your predator. Confrontation always escalates a situation. You want to identify if you are a target and then take the appropriate action to mitigate further aggression by reporting the incident or initiating your emergency contact plan. However, you must always be prepared to fight.

How do you expose a predator?

Once you identify a person of concern, look for that person in multiple disparate locations over a **significant** period of time. You must put **significant** distance and time between events to separate the coincidental from the intentional. This technique works whether you are in a car or on foot. The distance and time separation are simply compressed when on foot.

If you see the same odd behavior or person of interest in two separate locations over time, then you must confirm whether this activity is directed at you. You must quickly determine if you are becoming a target. Being especially watchful at this point, move to a different location over a longer period of time to draw out the predator. For example, if you are in your car and confirm that you have seen the same vehicle or person of concern multiple times in different locations, then make a final maneuver to draw out the predator. This is called provocation. In this case, distance is more important than time. Once you identify a potential threat you want to make a significant break from your normal pattern. Immediately put a few miles (this may be two miles in a densely populated city or 15 miles in a rural area) between you and the last sighting of the person of concern. Take the less-traveled and less-convenient roads. This tactic involves traveling on roads most people do not normally use if they have a purpose or a place to go. Transit a neighborhood instead of going around it on the main road. Make an occasional U-turn and look for your person of concern. Make an unexpected maneuver in your vehicle such as pulling over on the side of the road to briefly check your phone. Turn suddenly off your primary route (a couple of quick right-hand turns). All these maneuvers are meant to put the predator off balance and give you an opportunity to confirm that you are being targeted. These are maneuvers that no one is going to make, or attempt to keep up with unless they are stalking you. That is why it is called provocation. Your intent is to provoke a response from the predator that you can easily identify as nefarious. However, the objective is to do this in a non-confrontational fashion. You want to force the predator to expose himself; you do not want to confront the predator. Do not return home or drive to a family member's until you identify and mitigate the threat.

The same concept applies if you are on foot. However, remember you do not have the protection of a 4000-pound vehicle so do not put yourself in a position where you are isolated and become more vulnerable while you are trying to identify a predator. For example, if you are in the shopping mall and feel you are being stalked, walk relatively quickly to the far end of the mall, go to a different level if you are in a multi-level mall. This is something most people do not do when shopping. Most people stroll along, browse, and stop here and there. This action will force your person of concern to move with you, which will stand out. Take the person of interest into an area where they will not fit in and will be easily identifiable. Make a sudden stop in a ladies clothing or underwear store. This stop works whether you are male of female. What you want to avoid are common locations where anyone may randomly stop such as a coffee shop or computer store. Another example, if you are in a multi-level mall go into the high-end department store and immediately go to the back section of the top level farthest from the elevator or escalator. Browse the aisles while you watch for your person of concern to appear. This is an atypical action and requires a predator to react. If you do not see anything, return to the mall just as quickly, and on the same route. If someone is looking for you, you have essentially doubled back on them, and often this action startles the stalker into mistakes that you can then identify. These actions serve several purposes; the question regarding what is going on around you quickly gets answered, the thought process of the predator gets disrupted, and you give the predator momentary cause to reconsider his activities. As he reconsiders, he exposes his intentions. Again, do not confront the predator. Observe, record the details in your mind, and then take the necessary action to mitigate or escape the threat. Whenever you are on foot and exposed, you must always be prepared for immediate defensive action.

Active Shooter

An active shooter is someone actively engaged in attempting to kill people in a public setting like a mall, workplace, church, or school. In the grand scheme of things, your probability of encountering an active shooter is low. However, this does happen and is beginning to be a more frequent occurrence. Most companies do not have an active shooter plan. In fact, many companies do not even have fire evacuation plans. Therefore, it is your responsibility to have a plan and know what to do if an active shooter surfaces nearby or another emergency occurs. Most often, the threat will come from coworkers or their family members. Rarely, although it does happen, there are instances of random acts of violence from an outsider. You should always be alert to changes in circumstances and behaviors that could lead to a violent act. Awareness is fundamental to your survival in every circumstance. If you are aware of your surroundings and aware of subtle changes in those surroundings, you may spot a developing situation in time to get away from danger. Actions helpful in preparing you for danger are:

- Ensure that you know the two nearest exists in any building where you work or visit.
- Note aggressive behavior by someone who normally is not aggressive.
- Be aware of mood changes in others.
- Watch for those who display fits of anger over minor issues.

- Keep your ears open for talk by someone who wants to harm themselves or others.
- Be aware of threating emails or notes.
- Observe any unusual tardiness by fellow workers.
- Watch for employees who unnecessarily come and go from work during the workday.
- Be aware of those who brag about hurting people or getting revenge.
- Stay alert to alcohol or drug abuse by others around you
- Pay attention to anyone showing classic signs of depression.

According to the National Institute of Mental Health, symptoms of depression may include the following:

- o Difficulty concentrating, remembering details, and making decisions
- o Fatigue and decreased energy
- o Feelings of guilt, worthlessness, and/or helplessness
- o Feelings of hopelessness and/or pessimism
- o Insomnia, early-morning wakefulness, or excessive sleeping
- o Irritability, restlessness
- o Loss of interest in activities or hobbies once pleasurable, including sex
- o Overeating or appetite loss
- o Persistent aches or pains, headaches, cramps, or digestive problems that do not ease even with treatment

    o   Persistent sad, anxious, or "empty" feelings

    o   Thoughts of suicide, suicide attempts

Be aware that you are looking for differences—things that are not normal and are changes in behaviors and patterns. Such differences can indicate a developing problem. These differences can be subtle. In fact, it's not unusual to hear a witness or friend say, "He never showed any signs of aggressive behavior."

If you get caught in an active shooter scenario, your first action should be to evacuate the scene. Have an escape route in mind before you move, and help others to evacuate if possible. Should you be unable to evacuate, you should:

- Find a place to hide.
- Call 911, if it is safe, and leave the line open.
- Lock doors and windows.
- Stay out of the shooter's view.
- Get behind something that will provide some protection from bullets. For example, turn a desk on its side and get behind the desktop for protection. Get behind a file cabinet, or another heavy object.
- Do not get trapped. A room with windows provides options for evacuation, but a closet, although a good hiding spot, is a trap.
- Be prepared to take defensive action. Prepare to run or fight.

Violent Action as a Last Resort

If an assailant confronts you, you must react swiftly with violent, aggressive action. Use whatever is available to strike at the assailant. When you commit to defensive action, you must be as violent as possible. You

74

must attack with extreme aggression using your keys, fists, nails, or whatever weapon you have to deploy. Screaming as you mount your defense will help distract the assailant. It should not be a scream of fear; it should be a scream of anger and violence as you attack. Think of it as a war cry. The important point is to attack <u>violently</u>, <u>loudly</u>, and <u>relentlessly</u> until the assailant submits, leaves, or you can get away. In fact, the sheer violence of a defense can often be enough to cause an attacker to flee. Once forced into a defense, you must continue until you subdue your attacker, or you safely escape.

Emergency Planning

You should have an escape plan in the event of a natural disaster or criminal attack. Know the evacuation plan, routes, and rallying points for each building where you routinely conduct business.

Know your company's active shooter procedure, if they have one. Ensure you have a separate plan for your survival in the event of a shooter or otherwise disgruntled employee. Schools and businesses attempt to make their environments safe for their students, employees, and visitors, but ultimately the responsibility for one's security falls on the individual. In those moments during a disaster or physical attack, you are on your own. How well you prepare for such an event will determine whether you survive.

Emergency Survival Kit

Have an emergency or "go bag" that you keep at work, school, or other location where you may spend a lot of time (e.g., your car). Be prepared whether you work in a high-rise office building or a small storefront business in a strip mall. Bad things happen, disasters occur, and it is always necessary to be prepared. Based on individual circumstances, office location, and local climate, everyone's emergency bag will vary slightly. Take into account your particular circumstances when putting together your go bag. Ten items to have in a basic go bag are:

1. Small first aid kit that can fit in the palm of your hand and has a few Band-Aids, a pair of tweezers, antibacterial wipes, etc.

2. A flashlight or a small penlight and a whistle to draw attention in case of an assault or a medical emergency or natural disaster

3. A one-day supply of any critical medicine (insulin, nitroglycerin, etc.)

4. A written emergency phone list in the event your electronic device that stores all your data dies or is lost, this list should include the number to a local taxi service

5. Emergency cash that you do not touch except in an emergency (running out of beer does not constitute an emergency!)

6. Two protein bars and two pints of water (two 16-oz. bottles)

7. Small roll of duct tape (you can fix a lot of things with duct tape)

8. Space blanket

9. Small pocket knife

10. Backup battery for your cell phone, which you keep charged

Emergency Communications Plan

Establish an emergency communications plan with someone you trust. Regardless of the emergency, it is always good to have someone you can reach out to, send a message or a text to, and know that they will come or send you help. This plan should involve a prearranged agreement—not just that you phone a friend in an emergency. Establish duress words and a planned response. Your duress word should be something that will trigger your friend into action, even if you have not talked for a while. As your trigger, use a single word that you can fit into a sentence under any circumstance. For example, maybe your word is "dog" and you do not own a dog. Under duress or in a stressful situation, you may call your emergency contact and say something like, "I can't meet you tonight. The dog is sick and throwing up." To your contact, this triggers them to call the authorities, your parents, or your spouse/partner. An emergency contact plan is secondary only to calling 911. If you can dial 911, that should be your first call. However, in circumstances where you cannot make that call or the circumstances do not rise to the 911 level, you can still initiate your emergency communications plan. Maybe you are stuck at an office party, and your date is so drunk he or she cannot drive home. Maybe a coworker is stalking you. Always have a plan and a backup plan. Be aware of your surroundings and your conduct at all times.

Apply the common military principle of a PACE plan to everything you do because anything that can go wrong will go wrong at the worst possible time.

PACE: For every circumstance, you should have a:

- Primary Plan
- Alternate Plan
- Contingency Plan
- Emergency Plan

Stay In Touch

If you walk to work, school, or other activities, ensure that you walk with a buddy, especially if it is after dark or you have to transit through isolated areas of campus or town. We can repeat this message a thousand times: when you are isolated and separated from the herd, you become a target. If it is not practical for you to walk with a buddy, make sure someone knows where you are and where you are going at all times. Text a friend before leaving your dorm, house, or business to let them know you are leaving, where you are going, and what route you are taking. Check in with your friend when you get to your destination. We all do this every day, to varying degrees, by staying in touch with our friends and loved ones. You simply need to make a conscious decision to do this and have an agreed-upon plan of action. For example, when you leave your dorm room going to an evening class across campus, you should text your friend, "leaving for class, across the commons, and through the library." Your friend should acknowledge the text. You should both know about how long your trip will take. When you arrive at class, a simple "here" text and a "K" response signal that all is well. However, if your friend does not get a text indicating you have arrived in a reasonable amount of time, he or she should ping you and ask for your status. If no response, your friend should call the appropriate authorities. This may sound like a plan only for women, but in fact, everyone should have a similar plan. Anyone can fall prey to an accident, illness, or abduction. Survivability depends on early threat detection.

Personal awareness spans all aspects and circumstances of our lives whether man-made or an act of God. Being aware of your environment and always being prepared gives you an advantage in surviving an incident and in helping others to survive as well.

- Avoid altercation.
- Be prepared for physical attack (swift, violent action); take a self-defense course; always have a weapon available.
- Know the improvised weapons available to you in day to day life.
- Know and employ deception techniques.
- Know how to identify and expose a stalker or someone who is surveilling you.

☐ Have an evacuation plan for your home and any building you frequently visit.

☐ Have a survival kit available in the car, at work, and at home.

☐ Have an emergency communications plan with friends and family.

☐ Have a PACE plan for all major aspects of your life.

☐ _____

8 VULNERABILITIES IN THE HOME

Your home should be your castle—your haven from harm. Often, however, your home is a sieve, leaking information and fraught with vulnerability. The information in this chapter will help you assess the vulnerability within your home and help you identify those areas where you most need to focus your efforts regarding your safety.

Are You A Target?

We are all targets to varying degrees. It is important, however, to assess your vulnerability accurately so you can develop a security posture that you will adhere to and one that is within your available resources of time and money. As you begin to assess your risk, the first thing you need to consider is your public exposure. The degree to which you are publically exposed significantly impacts your risk. The higher your level of exposure, the more you must harden your posture of prevention. The less exposed you are, the more flexibility you have to accept some level of risk.

Are You Publicly Exposed?

For example, you are publically exposed if:

- You are a public figure, politician, or senior executive.
- All of your 1000 Facebook friends know where you live and when you go on vacation.

- You have been personally involved in public controversy or litigation (e.g., do you work in a business that was involved in legal issues or scandal in which you were publicly associated?).
- You belong to a social club or professional networking club.
- You are in a leadership position of a controversial charitable organization.
- You have, or have had, access to unique information as a result of being employed by the government or military.
- _____

Three Good Security Investments?

The three best investments in home security are a dog, an alarm system, and a fire-resistant safe.

Do you own:

1. A dog that barks at noises around the house? In this case, size does not matter. The bark is more important than the bite.

2. An alarm system that you actually use? Is your alarm system monitored? In case something causes your alarm system to trigger and you are away from home or are incapacitated, with a monitored system your monitoring service calls the authorities. However, if you cannot afford a monitoring service, it is very effective to have a loud siren installed both inside and outside your home. The siren draws attention and often scares off a thief. Always post one of the alarm company's signs in your window or your yard. This can be a bigger deterrent to a thief than the actual alarm itself.

    The single point of failure for a monitored alarm system can be the telephone line. If someone cuts the line or a disruption in service occurs to the line, you do not have a connection to the monitoring service. Most modern alarms have the add-on option of a cell phone backup. If the phone line goes down for any reason, the cell phone backup contacts the monitoring service.

It is also a good idea to turn on the window and door sensors even when you are at home. This way the sensors will alert you if anyone is attempting to enter your home. Keep the motion detector turned off to keep from continually setting off the alarm while you are in the house. Most modern alarm systems have a "Stay" and "Away" mode. The "Stay" mode will deactivate the motion and glass-break detector while you are in the home.

Make sure you know where your alarm's panic button is located, or if you have a remote FOB for a panic button, always keep it with you in the house. A triggered alarm generally initiates a phone call from the call center dispatcher who confirms the nature of the emergency. The beauty of the panic button is that, in addition to an immediate alarm siren, the call center immediately dispatches police before confirming via a phone call, a feature that reduces the police response time by several minutes.

According to FBI statistical reports, burglars typically spend less than 60 seconds breaking into a home and 30% of burglars enter the home through an unlocked door or window. The more difficult it is to gain access, the more likely a burglar is to reconsider the attack. Most convicted burglars (90%) say they would avoid a home with an alarm system and abandon home entry/attack if they encounter an alarm.

3. A fireproof safe to store important papers? A nice feature to have in your home is a fireproof safe or lockbox that allows you to keep important documents, emergency cash, and valuables safe from both burglars and fire with minimal investment. Ideally, you want a safe that is fire-resistant for 30 minutes and bolted to the floor or the wall. The smaller the safe, the more important it is to mount it to a fixed structure in the home to ensure a burglar can't simply pick it up and cart it off. You can purchase a small, 6-cubic-foot safe for less than $200 and provide significant protection for your valuables and your PII. A fireproof lock box is adequate for protecting important papers from a fire. During a theft, however, if the burglar locates the lock box, he usually steals it because of the presumption that it contains valuables.

Based on your physical circumstances and financial resources, one or all of these investments can make a significant difference in securing your home and your valuables.

Is Your Garbage a Vulnerability?

Garbage, the outer-most perimeter of the home. Predators, just like the police, collect information from your trash, including information that can be used to steal your identity or to incriminate you. What goes curbside or in the community dumpster should be nothing more than household garbage (e.g., milk cartons, bags, scraps, bottles, and cans). Anything with PII should be shredded or burned. There are many good, legitimate shredding services available. If you are looking for a commercial shredding company, ensure they are licensed and bonded. If you choose to use one of these services instead of doing your own shredding, then you need to remember that there is a vulnerability to insider threat and subpoena. The level of concern should dictate, but as long as you control your information and its disposal, you are eliminating the vulnerability. Additionally, if you buy a good crosshatch shredder, you can use the shredding as mulch for gardens and flower beds.

Do you put junk mail in your garbage? Junk mail, though not inherently compromising, allows anyone targeting you to know your interests and often your financial condition. If your discipline will allow, it is always best to dispose of junk mail through a shredder, shredder services, or by burning it. This action may not always be practical, but if you can get into the habit of shredding your junk mail, this action significantly reduces your outside exposure. In reality, will you shred every piece of junk mail you receive? No! But if you don't, you then must analyze every piece of mail, determine what could contain PII, and segregate it for proper disposal. For example, in all likelihood, you will throw away, in your regular garbage, the Sharper Image catalog with your name and address on the back cover. However, you may shred the promotional mail from United Airlines that clearly states on the outside of the envelope that you are a preferred member and your mileage plus cardholder status. Therefore, the easy answer is never to put any junk mail in your everyday garbage.

Do you dispose of bill receipts or check stubs in your regular garbage? Bill receipts and check stubs, for example, are all identifiers of your patterns of life and part of your PII. You must make a decision as to whether these are the indicators you want to leave behind. Remember, you want to develop two patterns in your life. The in-pattern life, which everyone sees (e.g., the garbage man, anyone watching your credit cards, all creditors, and the general public) and the out-of-pattern life, which has no physical or virtual connection and provides a place to do your most personal business. Do you want everyone to know where you bank or what prescription medicines you take?

Does your trash go curbside so that it is identified with your house or does it go in a common dumpster used by many? Common dumpsters are good and make a lot more work for someone who is searching your trash. Your trash is mingled with that of others, and for the average bad guy, it is harder to exploit and makes you a more difficult target. Many people do not put their trash curbside but take it to local dumpsters around town or the local dump and drop it off. These are effective ways to dispose of your trash, but not at all efficient. What you want to do is develop a plan and lifestyle that balances effectiveness with efficiency, and remains simple to execute. You can be very secure, but if your security consumes your every waking moment and is not efficient, you will simply cheat.

Do you own and use a shredder for all of your PII trash? Shredders are relatively inexpensive these days, and you can purchase one at many of the big box stores for less than $100. Do you own and use a shredder for disposing of all junk mail? You may view this as excessive, but if you shred your PII, why not go ahead and shred everything?

How Should You Handle Your Mail?

Your mailbox contains fantastic, personally identifying information. Ideally, it is best to have a P.O. Box at the local post office and receive mail there. Always mail letters and bills at the Post Office or by placing your mail in one of the blue Postal Service mailboxes. Never leave bills and letters in your mailbox for pickup. Every thief knows this is where you can find checks and various PII around the first of every month. If you need a physical address because of the type of packages you may receive, a box at the local UPS or FedEx store is the next best thing. This precaution significantly reduces the chances of having your mail stolen or exploited. When evaluating your security posture, you must determine what is suitable for your individual risks and determine if the cost is worth the gain in security. To send and receive all your mail at the U.S. Post Office may be secure, but depending on your proximity to the local post office, your neighborhood demographics, and your overall public exposure, it may be impractical or unnecessary. An alternative is to maintain a mailbox for only sensitive communications and receive your normal day-to-day mail at your home. That way you do not need to check your mailbox daily.

Should You Own A Firearm?

Do you own guns? This question may lead you to think we are suggesting you own a gun for home protection. In this case, that is not the intent of the question. Though a gun can be an excellent self-defense tool, it can also be a target for thieves. Is it common knowledge you have a weapon? One of the great mistakes people make is bragging about their weapons. No one needs to know you have a collection of pistols and rifles. Transparency, in this case, is not an advantage.

Are your weapons secured? A safe is the preferred method of securing firearms and weapons that are not in immediate use. When locked in a safe, your firearms are not visible, and they are much harder to steal. A variety of safes is available on the market ranging in size and protection ratings for fire and theft. Prices start about $200. You can purchase them at most gun and home improvement stores.

If you do not have a safe or space or resources to acquire one, at a minimum, you should put a trigger lock on any firearm that is not in immediate use or your possession. You can purchase trigger locks for $30—$50, which ensure your firearm(s) are not misused.

If you store your firearms in a portable lock box or decorative gun cabinet, you should always use trigger locks on the individual weapons, as well. A portable lock box is easy to cart off, and a thief can open it with a crowbar in a matter of seconds. Also, a thief can quickly penetrate your decorative gun cabinets, though affixed to a structure in the home, fully exposing your weapons to theft.

Do you have a good lighting system around your home?

Good lighting can be a significant deterrent to a predator. Remember, a predator is only effective if he can remain hidden until it is time to strike. A burglar's goal is to gain access in less than 60 seconds. The longer he is outside trying to get in your house, business, or car, the longer he is exposed. One of the best deterrents around the outside of the home is good lighting. Floodlights that are always on after dark are the best deterrent. However, this may not always be practical, especially in dense areas like townhomes and condominiums. Another good option is to install motion-sensor lights outside your house and keep shrubs and bushes cut back to prevent their use as a hiding place for a burglar. If you live in a townhouse or condo, install motion-sensor lights on the patio or on any external wall where there are windows or doors. Lights are just another feature you can employ to ensure better home security. Placing lights around your home's perimeter or at the external openings of your home is an immediate warning to intruders that you are concerned about your safety and security. Lights can also alert a passerby and draw attention to any unusual activity. You can now buy battery-powered smart lights that activate only in the dark and use LED technology to provide bright, white light that is portable and easy to install. You can purchase these lights starting about $15 from most home improvement stores.

How Aware Are You of Your Surroundings?

Personal awareness is a full-time endeavor. Whenever you step out into the world, you need to be alert. When you enter and exit your car, even in the garage or driveway, be on guard. When you walk out to get into your car, look around as you approach the car for anyone nearby. Do they belong there? Are they familiar to you? Be prepared to retreat into the house if you feel threatened. When you return home, before you even unlock your car doors, look around the area where you park. Look for anything out of the ordinary—things that look out of place or unusual— and anyone that may be unfamiliar and loitering too close to your location. When you exit your vehicle, have your key fob in your hand ready to push the panic alarm if someone approaches you or attacks you. Make sure you always lock your car, even in the driveway or the garage. This will help prevent someone from getting in your car and lying in wait to attack you.

Keep home doors and windows locked at all times, whether you are at or away from home. Though this advice is obvious, we all like to open up the house to get fresh air when the weather is pretty. This action, however, creates a risk—a point of entry for the predator. In determining the tolerance for this risk, you must consider the neighborhood in which you live, whether you have a dog in the house, whether you live on the ground floor, and whether you have alarms on your screens so you could open the windows but set the alarm for the screens. Opening the windows and the doors or leaving them unlocked gives a predator an easy route into your home. Such activity may even make you a target of opportunity for an otherwise unlikely burglar. You need to be a hard target, one that <u>never</u> presents an irresistible opportunity for a predator.

Be especially cautious when leaving a garage door code or alarm code with domestic help. Although convenient, and you may completely trust the service you use, those codes are often kept in your file at the cleaning service office where everyone has access to them. Ideally, you want to employ rolling codes for your guests—codes that can be used once and then changed. This can be cumbersome to manage, so a good rule is to change the garage and alarm codes you give to any guests or domestic help at least monthly. Your primary code can remain the same unless you have reason to believe it has been compromised.

If you have a doggie door for a medium-to-large-size dog, you need to be aware it is an entry point into your home that is not wired to your alarm system. If you leave your house, and the dog is not present, such as at the kennel, make sure you close and lock the doggie door. Taking this action will prevent other animals from getting into your house while you are away, in addition to preventing entry by thieves.

Intrusion can take many forms. It can involve an invited guest into your home who then turns aggressive; it can involve someone who breaks into your home, or it can involve someone who violates your personal space in the virtual world.

Be cautious when you answer your door at home. Make sure you have a peephole installed in the door so you can see who is knocking. NEVER answer the door for anyone you are not expecting or do not recognize. It is not a good idea to open the door with the chain attached to see who is there. The chain is nothing more than a mechanism to make you feel secure. A predator can easily overcome the chain with minimal force.

Keep a can of pepper or wasp spray by the front door for those circumstances where you may have to open the door for someone you do not recognize, like a delivery person or a utility person. Keep the can of pepper spray in your hand, ready to deploy if the person is aggressive. It is also a good idea to keep several cans of pepper or wasp spray strategically placed around the house, so in the event of an intrusion, you have something nearby to use to defend yourself.

Consider having a remote panic button for the house, one you can wear around your neck that connects to your main alarm system via radio signal. A panic button is especially useful for children and the elderly.

You should have a fallback or retreat position in the event of an intrusion. Your retreat position should be a safe room prepared for a defensive posture and your survivability. You can harden this room using reinforced doors, or you can simply designate a particular room in your home you have prepared accordingly. Your safe room should be a place in your house away from the primary entry points, preferably with only one exterior wall, one door, and a window for escape. In the safe room, you should keep the following:

- A phone to call for help.
- A device you can use to bar the door. A portable door brace is perfect, which you can purchase at any home store.
- A weapon of some type to mount a final defense, which may be any or all of the following:
  - Pepper or wasp spray; it is always best to have an incapacitating agent and a weapon available for follow through
  - Baseball bat, golf club, or other club like weapon
  - A large knife like a kitchen knife, or fireplace poker, or
  - A gun, preferably a shotgun or a revolver

In the event an intruder gets into your house, or you feel the entry is imminent, press your alarm's panic button or call 911 if you do not have a panic button, retreat to the safe room in your house, and bar the door. Assume a defensive position in the safe room and wait for the police to arrive. If you have a gun, get as far away from the door as possible and keep the gun aimed at the door. If you have another means of defense, you should be close to the door to mount an immediate and surprise attack if the intruder makes it through the door. Tell the 911 operator where you are in the house and if you have a gun. This information is important to the police when they respond and try to sort out who's who at the scene.

What Should You Know About Fire?

One of the cheapest forms of home safety is a smoke detector. Place smoke detectors in all bedrooms and one in the central portion of your home. If you do not wire your smoke detectors into the main house alarm system, make sure you change the batteries yearly. If you are unable to change the batteries, most local fire stations will send someone over to put them in for you. All you have to do is call them.

Keep a fire extinguisher handy in the house. Having a chemical extinguisher that you can use on electrical and grease fires is best. Keep the extinguisher in a central location in your home; if you have multiple floors, there should be one on every floor. Check the fire extinguisher yearly, and replace it as necessary, including when you check the tag and discover the extinguisher has expired.

It is important to have an evacuation plan in case of an in-home fire. Some of the factors to consider when making your evacuation plan, depending on where you live, are the time of day the fire occurs and outside weather conditions. If you live in a one-story, single-family home in southern Florida, you can afford to be a little less cautious. If you live in a multi-story home in Wisconsin, or in a high-rise condo in Denver, you will need to prepare for several evacuation scenarios. Consider the following as you plan your evacuation:

- Ensure that you have a smoke detector in all bedrooms and one centrally located in your house. A smoke detector is the single-most important piece of your evacuation plan, early warning.
- Keep a phone by the bed and keep your panic alarm with you at all times in the house.

- Have a small emergency bag packed and ready to go in the event of a fire. Ready to go means by the bed or centrally located so that you know exactly where it is. The bag should contain:
  o Flashlight
  o Protein bars for the family
  o Water
  o Knife
  o Backup supply of prescription medications you cannot be without for an extended period
  o Clothes for every member of the family, to include coats, hats, and gloves appropriate for weather conditions

Medical Emergencies

In a medical emergency, such as a heart attack or stroke, your survivability goes up significantly when you call an ambulance rather than drive yourself to the hospital. The first responders can begin applying time-critical aid when they arrive, and generally, your care at the hospital will begin immediately upon arrival in the ambulance.

It is also a good idea to have all members of the family attend basic first aid training and yearly refreshers. Many local governments provide first aid classes as a community service.

Natural Disasters

Whether you are plagued with wildfires and earthquakes in California, tornados in the mid-west, or hurricanes in the coastal states, disaster can occur with little notice. Preparation is key to survival. Though government services like police, fire and rescue, and FEMA assist during and after a natural disaster, it is important to understand your survival ultimately depends on you. No matter where you live, you should be prepared for survival without infrastructure for a minimum of seven days. If you have the resources, it is best to prepare for a minimum of 21 days without infrastructure support. This does not mean you have to go full Prepper and stock up for the Zombie Apocalypse. What this does mean is being prepared for the eventualities that happen every year across America. There are fires, floods, water contamination, toxic spills, a thousand things that can impact the safety of you and your family that have nothing to do with nefarious behavior. Things that just happen.

There are some companies that offer freeze dried food and packaged water that will last for 25 years in storage. This is obviously a good option. You can purchase a fixed supply and never have to worry about restocking unless you have to use the supplies. If the 25-year vittles and water are a little too hardcore for you, there are some very practical things you can do to be prepared for survival outside the infrastructure for some period of time.

- Get a small generator that can run a window air conditioner or other appliances like the refrigerator, or freezer.
- Have one gallon of water available per person per day of preparation for drinking and cooking.
- Food is tricky because we all have different tastes, allergies, and proclivities. However, remember you are preparing for an emergency, not a neighborhood cookout. Canned vegetables and meats provide the most flexibility. Boxed pasta and rice are also good alternatives, but there is still some preparation necessary whereas canned goods, in the worst case, can be eaten straight out of the can. Keeping things simple keeps cost down and waste to a minimum. For example, as a guide consider the following, modify as appropriate to your lifestyle:
  - Two cans of vegetables per person per day of preparation.

o   One can of starch, like potatoes or beans, per person per day.

o   Three, 6-8 ounce cans of meat per person per day. This can be chicken, turkey, sardines, Spam, etc. However, never lose sight of the fact that all canned goods, especially meats, can be high in sodium and fat. Choose wisely, choose low sodium and low fat when possible.

- If you lose power, use the generator to run your refrigerator and freezer for two hours every eight hours to keep your food viable. Consume what is in the refrigerator and freezer before you begin to dip into the emergency canned supplies. These stores can often carry you for many days if you have a generator. They can remain viable up to 48 hours without a generator.

- Ensure you have an alternative means of cooking. For example, even if you don't like to grill out, have a grill, charcoal or gas, and keep all the necessary supplies for operation as part of your preparation kit. You will need the grill to cook what is in the refrigerator or freezer. A small camping grill with a supply of propane gas canisters is best and can be used indoors, if necessary, like a gas stove.

- Have battery operated emergency lights, and a battery operated radio. Don't forget the batteries. Lights and radios that can be hand powered are preferred. Hand-powered devices reduce the reliance on maintaining a very expensive battery supply.

- If you have enough notice, make sure all vehicles are fully fueled, and you have at least three gallons of fuel for your generator per day of preparation. In an emergency, water and gas are the two things most sought after.

- Remember, if you are prepared you are also a target for those who are not.

Every year or so, based on your resources, you can donate your stores of food to a local homeless shelter and restock with fresh goods. Or, you may choose to use stored water and fuel on a rotating basis and replenish to keep stocks at sufficient levels.

Preparation does not have to be onerous. Make a list and work gradually to build up your position, so you are prepared and don't have to panic when there is an emergency. Regardless of the crisis you should have a plan for sufficient:

- Food
- Water
- Fuel
- Communications

What Are Your Plans for Your Defensive Posture?

Our defensive posture is our last stand; it is a defensive assault or call for help. You must have a plan for your defensive position. You should go over this plan with the entire family every 60 - 90 days, assign responsibilities to each family member, and make sure everyone understands what to do in the event of:

- Intrusion
- Fire
- Medical Emergency or
- Natural Disaster

AREA OF VULNERABILITY
The Home

Use the following checklist to break down the broad area of the home into subsystems or vulnerabilities.

Identify those things that are vulnerable to attack:
- ☐ Your profile
- ☐ Garbage
- ☐ Mail
- ☐ Wi-Fi
- ☐ Guns
- ☐ Your children
- ☐ _____

Identify those things that you are vulnerable to:
- ☐ Home invasion
- ☐ Fire
- ☐ Medical emergency
- ☐ Domestic help
- ☐ Heavy neighborhood crime
- ☐ _____

PDD™ CHECKLIST
The Home

Now that you understand some of the vulnerabilities and risk mitigation options regarding physical security in the home, use the following checklist to begin developing your security posture.

Prevention: What can you do to prevent becoming a target?
- ☐ Maintain a low profile
- ☐ Put only household garbage curbside
- ☐ Maintain an out-of-neighborhood mailbox for private communications
- ☐ Shred junk mail
- ☐ Shred all PII-related mail and documents
- ☐ Put a security alarm sign in your window or yard or both
- ☐ Have guest garage or alarm codes that expire
- ☐ Keep doors and windows locked at all times
- ☐ _____

Deterrence: What can you do to deter an attack once you become a target?
- ☐ Have a dog that barks
- ☐ Have an alarm system and use it
- ☐ Have a safe or fireproof lock box
- ☐ Secure your weapons
- ☐ Install external lighting
- ☐ Keep shrubs cut back
- ☐ Find a safe place to park
- ☐ Install cameras in/around the home
- ☐ Employ deception techniques to increase your defensive appearance
- ☐ _____

Defense: What can you do if you are attacked?
- ☐ Be prepared for a physical attack; take a self-defense course
- ☐ Keep weapons available throughout the house within easy reach
- ☐ Have a remote panic alarm for the house
- ☐ Have a rehearsed emergency plan for intrusion, fire, and medical emergency
- ☐ Place multiple fire extinguishers around the house

☐ Install smoke detectors in all bedrooms and the main living area
☐ Identify a safe room
☐ Have an evacuation kit available near your primary emergency exit
☐ _____

9 VULNERABILITIES OUTSIDE THE HOME

This chapter addresses vulnerabilities outside the home in a broad sense and defines techniques you can use to protect yourself from predators whether you are going to work or on vacation. The focus will be on simple, universal principles that are always applicable no matter your destination or mode of transportation. Personal awareness is a state of mind you should practice across all aspects of life. Something you never imagined can happen in the blink of an eye. Look at every circumstance as it develops knowing you are as prepared as possible.

Credit and Debit Card Cautions

There have been countless robberies at ATMs. You are the perfect target while retrieving money from an ATM. All the predator has to do is wait for you to come to the "watering hole." At an ATM, the predator can realize maximum benefit for minimal effort. Robberies at an ATM can take several forms. The predator can wait nearby until the machine dispenses the cash and then simply push you as a distraction, grab the money, and run. Then there is always the classic armed robbery. At knife or gunpoint, the predator approaches you at the ATM demanding your card and PIN number. Your hands are occupied, and you are distracted with what you are trying to do, all of which makes you extremely vulnerable. Remember you should always practice good security when getting cash from an ATM, because a predator could appear and rob you in the blink of an eye. A few tips to keep in mind while at an ATM:

- Never use freestanding ATMs, especially at night. Even the light of day will not deter a determined thief.

- Use an ATM inside a bank, grocery store, or convenience market, if possible.

- Always be aware of your surroundings, including anyone who might be around when you are at the ATM. Stay in view of the camera positioned at the top of the machine. If someone approaches you, the camera will catch his or her image also.

- Set a low per day withdrawal limit on your debit and credit cards to prevent a robber from cleaning out your bank account before you can cancel your card.

Credit card skimmers pose another huge problem. We have all heard stories about debit card use at the local convenience store gas pump. Once you insert your debit card into the gas pump machine, an electronic skimmer, placed there by a thief, records all PII stored on the card's magnetic strip. This information includes the card's number, expiration date, and security code from the back of the card and is all anyone needs to use your card to make purchases or to establish other forms of credit. This skimming device can be set up on virtually any credit or debit card machine, although the predator has to make an effort to attach the skimmer to the swiping mechanism.

Radio Frequency Identification (RFID) chips that are embedded in the credit card are becoming more common and soon will be ubiquitous. You do not swipe these cards; they are passed over or through a sensor. The problem with these cards is that a predator does not even need to touch the card or have it swiped. He just has to get close enough to you for his sensor to acquire your card's data. If you have RFID-enabled cards, you may consider using a wallet that is made specifically to protect against outside collection of your information. These wallets are made of a fine metal material that blocks the RF signal. A good rule of thumb is that you should regularly search the Internet for the latest skimming scams and be familiar with how predators are changing their tactics as technology changes. New means of theft are created every day.

What Can You Do About Skimming Scams?

- Before swiping your card at a gas pump, inspect the area around the card reader. A sticker from the state or county that indicates the machine is calibrated will likely be nearby. Look for forced entry into the gas pump panel, and look for anything abnormal about the panel. A damaged or broken state or county certification sticker is your cue to avoid this machine. Because card skimmers must go to the trouble of inserting a device to extract data from your card, your safest payment method is to go into the store to pay for your gas or use the pump closest to the front door in full view of the attendant. Keep in mind that it is hard for the predator to penetrate these machines, so you need to make your purchase in a manner in which it is difficult for the predator to prevail. Cash is king, but cash is inconvenient and dangerous to carry if overseas, for example. Using your cards appropriately should be your objective.
- Use credit cards that can be sacrificed—those with a low-credit-limit for everyday use. Keep higher-value cards for emergencies in a safe location, maybe in a safe at home or safety deposit box. If you are traveling, keep these cards in an ankle wallet or other stash location.

Due to counterfeiting, many countries no longer take traveler's checks in exchange for currency, only new U.S. dollars for exchange. Before traveling overseas, make sure you research the countries' requirements, carry cash in new U.S. bills for exchange, and use a credit card that is being monitored for fraud. You can also use a preloaded debit card; however, there is no protection if you lose your card or the number is exploited. The card is like cash: it is gone with no recourse. By using a valid credit card with a fraud monitor on it, you do not lose anything if it is stolen or exploited.

Notify your financial institutions before you travel. They can flag your accounts to indicate you are traveling and your approximate travel locations. This action serves two functions: it keeps your cards from being deactivated because you set off the fraud alerts by being out of your normal pattern, and it ensures your cards will be monitored closely for fraud while you travel.

Tracking You through Your Credit Cards

There are many ways to track your location, one of which is through credit and debit card purchases. Efforts by the credit card companies to tighten up on fraud have initiated the use of some impressive technology and complex algorithms. However, that technology can also be used to track your whereabouts in near real time. Whether it is to verify your available credit for a purchase or to determine if the purchase fits within your normal patterns, credit card companies use a complex system to identify you, monitor your patterns, and track your location. Because all this happens at the time of the transaction, your purchase is posted online almost immediately. This feature also is beneficial because it helps you keep track of family members as the pending charges show up almost immediately online in your account activity. A good example is when your teen or young college student is supposed to be going on spring break in Ft.

Lauderdale, but you find out by monitoring their credit card purchases that they are really in New York. The charges show up online literally within seconds of the purchase going through.

Anyone having access to your online bank or credit card accounts will be able to see, almost in real time, where you are. This includes vehicle toll and parking garage transactions. Exploitation of this feature can happen in a number of ways to identify your patterns, proclivities, and habits. The only way to avoid this tracking is to use cash or preloaded debit cards.

Your Secret Stash:

Losing your credit cards or passport can destroy a vacation or business trip and leave you vulnerable. If you travel, even just a little, loss of your valuables is inevitable at some point. However, you can take some actions to reduce the damage caused by loss or theft. Consider purchasing an ankle or thigh wallet, or a wallet that hangs around your neck and is secure under your shirt, not one that hangs outside of your shirt. You should not consider this hidden wallet to be a convenience, but a means to secure an alternate supply of money, credit cards, and important documents. This wallet should contain the following emergency items:

- Emergency cash; the amount should be determined by location and duration of travel.
- Backup credit card.
- A photocopy of credit and debit cards you are carrying. (You should copy front and back, so you have both the account and contact information.)
- Photocopy of your passport and other relevant documents, driver's license, travel itinerary, etc.
- Emergency contact numbers.

The purpose of a secret or hidden wallet (or stash location) is to protect an emergency cache of money and contacts in the event you need them. It is just as important for you to protect the fact that you have an emergency cache as it is for you to have one in the first place. In addition to keeping quiet about your emergency stash, you should never access the contents of your leg or neck wallet in public. If you need to access your emergency stash, you should do so in a private location like a restroom. Always remember your stash is only for emergencies, and it is not a good idea to pull it out to buy a bottle of beer at the airport! If you are traveling through an airport, keep in mind that the security screeners will see the ankle or neck wallet on their body scanner and will want to see it and look inside, if not X-Ray. Be cooperative, show them the wallet, and then tuck it away.

To illustrate the importance of protecting your stash, a partner and I were in the Philippines during one of the many coup attempts in the early 1990s. We had been augmenting and providing additional on-the-ground support to the Agency officers stationed in the country. As the violence grew worse over several days and the armed rebels began assaulting government buildings and foreign interests, we got our orders to get out of the country as soon as possible. Authorities were starting to close the airport and only a few flights per day were leaving Manila. Once at the Manila airport, we would need to purchase a ticket, in cash, on whatever airline was flying out that day. At that time, it was common for us to carry several thousand dollars in cash as emergency "get home" money. I usually carried $5000 in different locations on my body. Before we left the office for the airport, I pulled out $2000 from my emergency stash and placed it in my front pocket, so it was handy but relatively safe. The Embassy travel officer had told us the ticket would be between $1500 and $2000 and because of the lock down the airlines were only taking cash.

When we got to the airport, it was deserted. A few foreigners were walking around trying to buy tickets, while the Pilipino soldiers providing airport security were guarding the entrances and exits. Otherwise, the place was devoid of activity. My partner and I looked for fights leaving the Philippines and found a flight departing for Los Angeles that afternoon. The Pilipino woman at the ticket counter was young and attractive with a pleasant smile in contrast to the relatively dismal surroundings of the empty airport. We requested two tickets on the afternoon flight to LA. She said the tickets would be $1500 each and there were plenty of seats available. I reached into my pocket and pulled out the money I had set aside and swiftly counted off $1500 in crisp $50-bills. (At the time, they preferred dollars to the Pilipino peso due to the terrible exchange rate.) While the woman printed my ticket and receipt, I looked over at my partner as he leaned against the ticket counter with one boot off and a sock in his hand from which he pulled out a wad of hundred-dollar bills. The attendant looked at him while he counted off 15, sweat-soaked, one hundred dollar bills as if he were an alien from another planet. When he reached out to hand her the soggy bills, she paused a long second before reluctantly taking the money. We got our tickets and walked away as my partner still wore only one boot, so much for keeping your stash hidden!

Planning is the key. You must see situations as they are developing and prepare for them before you need to react. If you wait to prepare until you need to react, you end up bootless in a foreign airport attracting undue attention to yourself.

Theft of Valuables

Pickpockets are prevalent worldwide, and we are all vulnerable to them. The following points of interest will help you reduce the risk of becoming a pickpocket's target.

- Wallets go in your front pocket, never in your back pocket or your suit jacket pocket.

- When in crowded areas, like foreign markets or busy streets, keep your hand on your wallet, and keep your purse or backpack between your wallet and the crowd.

- If you suddenly find yourself in chaos—a lot of talking, someone asking you to borrow your phone, or someone suggesting that you dropped something—this is your warning to lock down. Hold on to your items and put yourself in a defensive posture before reacting to the chaos. The chaos can often be a distraction while you are robbed.

- Your purse or backpack containing any valuables should be zipped closed. Remember, someone can cut your backpack or purse straps in the blink of an eye. Keep your bag close to you, preferably clutched between your body and your arm so you can hold on to it.

- Do not get distracted while you are paying for an item. You are the most vulnerable when your wallet is out, and your bag is open. Always keep a hand on your wallet and your bag in front of you in full view. Vigilance is the key! It only takes one distraction for a few seconds for your valuables to disappear. The predator will watch you, follow you, and see how attentive you are. If you present yourself as a hard target by the way you carry yourself and your valuables, the predator will move on to another target, one that is less prepared and aware.

- Carry a zippered purse or backpack, not an open bag. An open bag is an easy target for pickpockets, and items in the bag often fall out during movement. Keep your bag zipped when you are not accessing it.

- Carry your bag across your body, not over one shoulder. Hold backpacks in front of the body when in crowded areas. Carry your purse such that it hangs in front of your arm, not behind it. A purse hanging behind your arm is easier for a pickpocket to access, and the strap is easier to cut if you get bumped and prodded in crowded environments.

- Keep your wallet and phone in a side zipper pocket or at the bottom of your purse or backpack. This increases the effort required by the predator to steal these items.

- Never hang your purse, backpack, or bag over a chair, coat hook, or bathroom stall. If you take your bag off your body, place the strap under a chair leg or wrap the strap around your leg. This action is a significant deterrent to someone who might try to snatch your purse or backpack and run.

A large group of us was sitting in the city square at an outdoor café in Budapest just after the attacks on September 11, 2001. One member of our group was an Army Green Beret. His service took him all over the world, and he was well seasoned. He carried his backpack with him everywhere he went. The backpack contained all of his worldly travel possessions, passport, cash, wallet, and even his wedding ring he had secured while working out earlier in the day. The first mistake, NEVER keep everything needed for survival in one location and not losing your wedding ring is part of your survival. Upon pulling off his backpack, he hung one strap over the back of the chair where he was sitting. Several hours later, as we all got up to leave, he realized his backpack was gone. It had vanished. A passerby stole the backpack and all his possessions in broad daylight, in front of everyone in the group. No trace of the backpack was ever located. This story is a reminder that you must remain vigilant at all times. Remember, as a potential target or victim; you have to be on guard 100 percent of the time while the predator only has to be lucky once.

Social Settings

Parties, bars, and social events offer endless opportunity to be compromised. You should maintain a professional decorum at any function. This means not drinking excessively and suddenly deciding you know better how to run the company than the owner. It also means you should not be sexually inappropriate with coworkers, their wives or husbands, and superiors. Remember, in today's world, everything is recorded. At any given time, fully one-third of party attendees will have their phones out capturing video and pictures, and they can use these against you. You must form good habits beginning with the understanding that there are dangerous and disingenuous people in the world, who only look for the weak among us. They may use your actions to embarrass you and make you less competitive or to extort your bad behavior with your spouse or boss.

You can say, "it will never happen to me," but the road to Heaven is paved with the bodies of those who have uttered those words. Do an Internet search on "abductions" and read the articles about all of those who thought it would never happen to them.

Never leave your drink alone or with a stranger when you get up to go to the bathroom or go to the dance floor. It only takes a second for someone to drop something in your drink. If you are a young woman in a dance club full of young men on the prowl, you must be extra vigilant in watching what you drink and eat. Do not let a stranger bring you a drink. If someone buys you a drink, make sure a server brings it to you. You may ask why the responsibility falls on you to be so attentive. Right, and wrong have nothing to do with this topic. The truth is if you leave your drink alone, or you eat or drink something that not everyone is sharing, you become vulnerable. Most people are honest and kind, but predators leave us no option but to be prepared. Note that you may get lucky 999 times, but there will be that one time when you become a target. You must never get complacent simply because nothing has happened yet.

You should <u>never</u> leave a party or bar alone. It is always a good idea to have a buddy nearby should you drink a little too much, have some relationship drama, or simply want to go home. If you drink too much, you lose your inhibitions and common sense. No matter how big and tough you are, male or female, the buddy rule always holds true. You are a wounded animal in the eyes of a predator if you drink too much and get separated from your friends. All predators can smell weakness. Establish a buddy rule with at least one friend in your group with whom you trust. You and your buddy should agree on a plan that does not let either of you leave alone or with a stranger. Yes, this is a "prude" approach, and it is no fun. However, if you end up separated and alone, you are in danger! The probability that a predator will target you greatly increases.

Have an emergency contact in case you get into trouble or your primary plan collapses under the weight of reality. You should always have a couple of people you can call in an emergency. Have a plan for the 2:00 am call from the bar when you are afraid to go to your car because someone inside has been stalking you all night. Have options and backups in the event your first choice is not available. Remember PACE: Primary, Alternate, Contingency, and Emergency. The way the world generally works is that when you have no options, you will need one the most. Preparedness is the best deterrent.

Have a safe word or phrase established with your friends so if you get into trouble or trouble is developing; you can use the safe word—either in conversation, text or on the phone—to get help or to signal for assistance when leaving the scene. For example, if you are at a club with friends and everyone is dancing and mingling, you can easily get separated from your friends. With a safe word or phrase, you have a quick way to communicate danger. If you are talking with someone and they begin to be aggressive, or if you try to get away from them, and they follow you, you should try to text your safe word or phrase to your friends. Another option as you mingle with your friends from time to time is to work the safe word into your conversation with them, so they know you have a threat, and they need to keep an eye on you or get help. A safe word should be something that you would not normally use in conversation but to an outsider would seem completely normal. Your safe word might be "sister." Therefore, you might say, "I just remembered my sister is coming to town tomorrow, and I won't be able to go out." Your friends, of course, are aware that you do not have a sister and the use of this word "triggers" them into action.

When you are out socially, some simple changes in behavior can make a big difference in your safety and security.

- Never leave your drink alone or with a stranger.
- Never let a stranger bring you a drink. Make sure you only receive a drink from a server.
- Go to the bathroom with a buddy.
- Travel to and from business and social events with a buddy, if possible. If not, make sure someone knows where you are at all times. When you are in transit, ensure that someone knows what route you are taking.
- Do not discuss with strangers anything more than superficial details about your work, business, or personal travel plans or

any details about your family. Someone is always listening, and you never know to whom you may be talking.

Emergency Travel Kit

It is important to have an emergency kit when you are traveling. Your travel may be to Grandma's house through the haunted forest or overseas on vacation, but the essentials are the same. The following list provides some of the basic emergency kit items that never change (you can add or subtract items as you see fit).

- A small first-aid kit
- A flashlight
- A whistle
- Two protein bars
- Two pints of water (i.e., two, 16-oz. bottles)
- A space blanket
- A one-day supply of any critical medicine (e.g., insulin or nitroglycerin)
- A written emergency phone list in the event the electronic device storing your data dies
- A pen and small pad of paper

Blend Into Your Environment

Be considerate, dress appropriately for the area you are visiting. It is not a good idea to stand out as a tourist whether you are in Los Angeles or Latin America. If you are loud and obnoxious, you are making yourself a target. If you wear your Rolex watch and gold chain into a bazaar in Latin America, you are making yourself a target (i.e., do not be flashy in a subdued environment). Wearing flashy items like expensive clothes and jewelry when you are traveling makes you a target for several reasons.

- It draws attention to the fact that you have things of value. If a predator is looking for a target, you have now caught his attention.

- It is offensive to the locals because you may have items of value they do not have.

- A thief can steal your valuables for profit or spite. Know the environment you are visiting. You will never fit in like a local, but you can blend in from a cursory standpoint, and that is often enough to send the predator looking for a flashier target.

The James Bond Syndrome

The "James Bond syndrome" usually affects men but can affect women as well. The crux of the problem occurs when a man travels to a different city or foreign country and suddenly finds that he is irresistible to the gorgeous 20-something-year-old blond with the killer figure. The guy is often stricken with the notion that he is the personification of James Bond, which he thinks is normal for him. As a rule and <u>without exception</u>, when this happens the traveler is being targeted for something nefarious. If a gorgeous blond makes your acquaintance or a handsome man invites you for a ride in his Ferrari and such activities are out-of-the-norm in your everyday life, then you are a target. You are not that special just because you leave the confines of your state or country!

Some important points to note about becoming a target when you travel (and again they are almost universal and without exception).

- If it looks too good to be true, then it is not true.

- If you do not commonly experience this type of behavior, then you are a target.

- Do not ever honestly answer questions about your work, home, or family until you have thoroughly vetted the person to whom you are talking. Much like the cyber world, you can divulge small amounts of information that can be used to piece together a target package on you and your family. It is a good idea to have a generic story prepared in your mind for the casual encounter. For example, if you are in Amsterdam on business, and you work as a lawyer for a major shipping firm, consider a story line close to the truth but varied enough not to lead back to your real life. Someone who is targeting foreigners for theft or exploitation would find a lawyer for an international shipping company to be an appealing target. Your safe story should be something consistent with your training so you can speak intelligently about it while altering the details to make you a less attractive target. Maybe, in this case, you would pose as a pro bono attorney for the homeless who is just attending an international conference. Choose something benign, although this is a hard thing to do. When you work so hard to achieve success, you want to take every opportunity to brag about it, especially when conversing with the sexy girl or the handsome man you meet on an airplane. Be mindful that you can brag later when you have fully vetted the subject. Success automatically makes you a target.

- It is a good idea to establish a routine communication channel with your family or emergency contact. For routine communications, consider having a blind or throwaway email account from one of the major providers. Get a fresh, disposable account for both ends of communication for each trip; throw away the account and do not use it again after the trip ends.

- Do not use open Wi-Fi access points when accessing sensitive IP addresses, such as bank accounts, online shopping sites, or your home IP address.

- Use a voice over IP (VOIP) service for voice calls to your friends and family back home. Not only is this far cheaper, but it also reduces the risk of exploitation of your cell phone and keeps someone from eavesdropping on your conversation from a hotel phone. However, as previously discussed, technology is an aid, not a solution. Save any sensitive or compromising conversations for a face-to-face meeting.

Hotel Room Safety

Once you check into a hotel, you should become acquainted with your surroundings to help ensure your stay is safe (and the location of the mini bar is not paramount!). When you get to your hotel room:

- Locate the nearest building exit.
- Locate the nearest fire alarm pull box.
- Place your flashlight on the nightstand when you arrive. Check to make sure you even have a flashlight.
- Lay out a dress of clothes readily available while you sleep in case of an emergency, to include a coat if it is cold out. You would be surprised at the number of travelers who will evacuate their hotel rooms at 2:30 a.m. in 30-degree weather, barefooted, in their PJs, with no flashlight, and no identification.

- Pack a purse or small backpack with your valuables, including money and ID, to have handy so you can grab it and run in the event of an emergency.

- Use the deadbolt and security chain **whenever** you are in the room. It won't stop a determined predator but will buy you precious seconds to take a defensive posture. Always keep balcony doors locked.

- Never leave valuables or high appeal items in the room unattended. This includes your toothbrush. Disgruntled hotel staff have done some pretty disgusting things to personal hygiene items.

- You may find it convenient to use a hotel room safe for valuables you do not want to carry around routinely. You have to balance convenience with the fact that once you place your valuables in someone else's possession, they become vulnerable. Much like outsourcing the storage of your data. There are always "backdoors" or ways to bypass the locks on hotel safes. However, depending on the local crime rate, you may determine that your valuables are at less risk in the hotel safe than on the street with you. If you have a choice, use a safe at the front desk and get a receipt for what you are securing.

- You may be in a situation where there is not a safe or you must leave some of your things in the room unattended. There are complex concepts for "trapping" your room so you can know when someone has accessed the room and looked through your personals. However, in the modern age of cell phones and digital cameras, there are some easy steps you can take to enhance your awareness. You can digitally "trap" your room and belongings so you can at least be aware if you are being monitored or targeted. It is very easy and requires little preparation.

First, you should always place the "Do Not Disturb" sign on the door when you are out so you can differentiate between nefarious activity and room cleaning.

Second, go through your room quickly and take no more than six pictures of the orientation of those things that may be of interest to a predator. Six is a good number because if you try to document the whole room, it becomes a time-consuming effort with little return on investment. Photograph the orientation of your computer, maybe place an innocuous item like a napkin near or on the computer for context. Something that no one would consider if they slightly adjusted the position. Photograph the position of the zippers on your luggage and the position of your toiletry bag. When you return, compare the pictures you took to how you find the room. Even professionals find it difficult to return items close enough to the original location to defeat a picture.

A partner and I had returned from an extended trip to Africa. We had been gone for more than four months, living in the wild in the middle of one of Africa's lengthiest civil wars. We were American advisors to the rebels during a surrogate war with the Soviets. Because of the danger and threat of assault, we had developed a security posture that prepared us to run or fight at a moment's notice based on our circumstances. When we returned to the United States, we stopped in Washington, D.C., for debriefing. One night while staying at a 15-story hotel in nearby Virginia, the hotel's fire alarm went off about 3 a.m. Everyone began evacuating; it was cold in early November. Out in the street, the hotel guests were milling about, discussing what may have happened—women in robes, men in sandals and shorts. Families huddled together to stay warm. I moved across the street out of the crowd and in a position to observe the area. My partner walked up. We looked at each other and laughed. We were both fully clothed, had our coats on, backpacks strapped in with all our necessities, and our flashlights in hand. We could have walked away and never needed anything. I realized then how unprepared people are for something as simple as a fire or catastrophe in everyday life. Be prepared; be vigilant!

Airplanes, Airports, and Luggage - Some basic rules for air travel include:

- Do not buy tickets using cash unless there is no alternative; this flags you for additional scrutiny. Drug dealers and people that have things to hide use cash. If you need the purchase to be anonymous, buy a prepaid debit card with cash and use the card to purchase the ticket. Prepaid debit cards can be purchased through major retail outlets and directly from MasterCard or Visa. Though it is important to remember if you buy a prepaid card online, and use your bank account for the purchase, then you and your bank account are forever tied to that prepaid card number. The only way for the prepaid card to be truly anonymous is to purchase it with cash.

- Never put items in checked luggage you are not willing to lose. That is the rule, and that includes all of your electronic devices.

- Never pack all your belongings in one bag and fool yourself into thinking there is no way it will ever get lost. If you travel, you will lose your luggage at some point, and if you are lucky, it will eventually resurface—maybe. To ensure your vacation or business trip is not a bust, you should take a staggered packing approach, something that is a good security measure and very practical.

- Do not forget to have a carry on cabin bag with you, which should include:
  - o Your valuables—jewelry, computer, phone, etc.
  - o Emergency kit
  - o Two days of clothes that can be washed into four days of clothes
  - o Basic toiletries
  - o All your medications—these should be in a carry on bag in their original bottles with your name and the prescription information. Many police officers, both domestically and abroad, will flag you for further investigation if you have unidentified medicine in your bag or your car.

- Do not put your full name and address on your luggage, and never display business cards. Put only your first name and your cell phone number on your luggage. Never, EVER, put your home address on your luggage. If you have to use an address, use a business address or your personal mailbox.

- Every "expert" has an opinion on where you should sit on a bus, train, or airplane. It is often hard to get the exact seat or location you may want. The one thing you should focus on when choosing a seat is being near an exit. The closer to an exit the better. Familiarize yourself with evacuation procedures before departure and prepare, in your mind, for your reaction in the event of an emergency. You do not want to get trapped.

- In taxis, private cars, or ride sharing services it is customary to sit in the back seat on the passenger side. However, sitting behind the driver gives you a tactical advantage in the event the driver becomes the predator. Whenever you are in proximity to an unknown individual you want to position yourself favorably to mount a defense or attack in the event you become a target.

Your Vehicles

For many of us, our vehicle is a second home. We use it to commute, to store various necessities we cannot live without when away from home, and as a catchall for things that have no real place in the rest of our lives. Unfortunately, the things we leave in our car tell the outside world a great deal about who we are and how attentive we are to the details of our lives.

A predator looks for things that will give him an advantage when pursuing a target, such as a plane ticket, a credit card receipt, or even an open planner that may indicate where the individual will be at a particular time. The predator uses this information to target the individual or to know when their residence is vacant so they can strike. The predator looks for things to prey upon—indications of weakness or vulnerability. Leaving items like house keys, money, work identification, or electronics in your car's console or in plain view is an invitation to a predator. The best-case scenario is that a predator breaks into the vehicle and steals only objects of value. The worst-case scenario is that the predator targets you for home invasion or abduction. Additionally, never leave PII behind as trash when you return a rental car (e.g., boarding passes and hotel, gas, and restaurant receipts).

Do not connect your cell phone via Bluetooth to your rental car's audio/phone system. Use a personal Bluetooth headset or a wired headset instead. Delete all data you have stored in the car's navigation system before returning the car. Be a hard target.

Just about everyone who drives has been told, at one time or another, to drive defensively. What you need to do is to drive with awareness and prepare for offensive action. Put down your distractions, especially in unfamiliar environments. Be aware of developing circumstances that may lead to an accident or assault. You must pay attention at all times. When you are driving and moving around in the world, the dynamics are constantly changing. For instance, you may stop at a traffic light next to a thug in a wife-beater who is loudly playing his gangster music and trying to look menacing. How you act for those few seconds at the traffic light can determine whether you become a target. Do you appear aggressive or just alert? Whether male or female, you want to appear aware and alert but disinterested and non-aggressive at all times. Keep in mind, in all circumstances aggression escalates the situation. There may be times when aggressive behavior is necessary, but in most daily interactions, you should just interact with others around you as appropriate and move on to the next activity in your life. While you are in your car, it is important to maintain a non-aggressive persona, because a large percentage of assaults, both premeditated and circumstantial, occur when you are driving.

- Be aware of your surroundings.
- Be non-aggressive with your behavior when driving.
- Be prepared for evasive or offensive action.
- Present yourself as a hard target.
- Keep the inside of your vehicle clean and tidy. Lock high-appeal items like computers, phones, and cameras in the trunk. Leave nothing exposed for a predator to steal or exploit.
- If you have a vehicle without a trunk, like an SUV, it can be difficult to get your valuables out of sight. Carry several black

bath towels or sheets to cover whatever you must leave in the vehicle. In the back seat or the cargo area, even under a streetlight, it's hard to see anything covered with black cloth.

- Park in well-lighted areas where there is substantial public foot traffic. Be self-aware. Check your mirrors and look around the perimeter of your vehicle before you unlock the doors to exit. When entering your car, immediately lock the doors. Do not wait for your doors to lock automatically once you drive away. When you are in a parking lot approaching your car, do not get distracted by talking on your cell phone or texting. Be aware of anyone getting too close or trying to get your attention. In these circumstances, an assailant can be on you before you have fully processed the threat. Keep your keys in your hand and use them as both a weapon and an alarm by pressing the panic button on the key fob, which will set off the car alarm. This action attracts attention and will often scare off an assailant.

- Do not use a valet service to park your car. As previously discussed, once you turn over your keys to an unknown individual, you have compromised the integrity of your vehicle and your belongings inside. Modern vehicles are primarily just complex computer systems, convenient but imminently subject to hacking. Depending on your public exposure, using a valet can vary from low risk to very high risk. If you are a public figure or senior executive, you should never leave your vehicle with unknown individuals. As a public figure, you are always a target, and you must minimize your exposure where possible.

Traffic Stops

Know the local laws. Some states have laws against texting and driving, while other states have laws on the use of earphones. For example, most states allow you to use a single headphone, but if you have both ears covered it is a violation.

If possible, ask for a rental car displaying a license plate from the state where you will be traveling. There is an old wives' tale that the police target vehicles with out-of-state plates. Whether this is true is debatable, but what is undeniable is that you make yourself less visible in a car displaying tags of the state you are visiting. Remember, the objective is to be a hard target; do not flag yourself as a target. The same is applicable in traffic stops. You could argue that you should not have to show your hands if you are doing nothing wrong. However, the reality is, if you don't show your hands in good faith, a police officer may categorize you as a threat regardless of your race, age, or ethnicity. Your objective should be to lower the threat concern in the officer's mind during a traffic stop.

When being stopped by the police, it is important to conduct yourself appropriately. If the police officer feels comfortable in the situation, there is often less confrontation involved. Several things you need to consider during a traffic stop are:

- Take out your driver's license and insurance card. Put both hands on the steering wheel. If the police officer can see your hands, his security posture is immediately more relaxed.

- If you have passengers in your car, they should take their hands out of their pockets, put down any electronic devices, and sit quietly.

- Roll down your window just far enough to hand the officer your license and communicate. Do not unlock your doors until you fully understand the situation.

- Do not offer any information to the officer and answer questions only when asked.

- Notify the officer if you have a concealed weapons permit and a weapon in your car.
- If the police officer is in plain clothes or in an unmarked vehicle, ask to see identification or credentials before unlocking or exiting your vehicle.
- If you feel threatened by the process, call 911 and leave the line open.

Traffic Lights and Congestion

When you come to a stop in traffic, leave enough space between you and the car in front of you in case you need to escape, a car length is not too much. Always be aware of your surroundings and look for an escape route when in heavy traffic. It is important to leave some maneuvering room if you need to escape from trouble or if you need to use your car as a weapon against an attacker.

Road Rage

Road rage can escalate quickly with little provocation. The simple rule is, do not engage. Once you engage, no matter how manly you are, the situation will inevitably escalate. If you are involved in a road rage incident, do not go home. This action identifies, to your aggressor, where you live and makes your whole family vulnerable. Instead, drive to the nearest police or fire station. Do not get out of your vehicle. You have a much higher probability of survival inside your car than outside your car. Also, as a last resort, you can use your vehicle as a weapon. If someone gets out of their car and comes over to you in anger, prepare yourself for defensive action, whether it is leaving the scene or getting out the pepper spray in case the aggressor breaks the window. Then dial 911, give the operator the details and your location, and leave the line open. Never get out of the car, this only escalates the situation.

Remember, if you are in your car, you have a 4000-pound weapon at your fingertips. Unless you are trapped in traffic, or the vehicle is on fire, you are usually better off remaining locked in your vehicle.

Flat Tire or Mechanical Trouble

Remember, prevention is the best strategy. Always maintain your vehicle and have life safety and emergency systems corrected immediately. Before a road trip, get your car inspected for dangerous or impending mechanical issues. This preventative action helps to ensure you will not have to attempt repairs on the side of the road. Several options to reduce your exposure to predators and reckless drivers are:

- Check the air pressure in your tires regularly, including the spare tire. We all forget to check the spare until we need it. Under inflation is one of the primary reasons for tire failure.

- Sign up for a roadside assistance rider attached to your car insurance policy. These are often relatively inexpensive and can pay for themselves with one flat tire. If you cannot afford a roadside assistance policy, sign up for private services like AAA and AARP. These services can provide quality roadside assistance at affordable prices and often offer other benefits like discounts at hotels and restaurants. Additionally, many car manufacturers offer roadside assistance during the vehicle's warranty period.

- Research complimentary roadside assistance which is provided by most states on the main highways and interstates. Roadside assistance is usually administered by the state highway patrol. Know the phone number of your state's roadside assistance service before setting out on a trip. Be sure to record and carry with you the phone numbers for roadside assistance in the states where you will be traveling. These numbers are posted online.

- Pull your car completely off the road onto the shoulder, if possible, should your vehicle have a mechanical failure.

- Exit the vehicle and move away from the road if you are stranded on a busy road and the weather will allow. This action will help protect you from reckless or inattentive drivers. Viewing just one episode of Crime Stoppers or Real Cops that shows the inattentive driver plowing into a police vehicle or a stranded motorist on the roadside should make you aware how cautious you should be.

Wildlife

Animals are the biggest threat to a driver when traveling on rural roads. What can you do to increase your survivability when in an area dense with wildlife?

- Slow down and proceed at "survival speed." When driving through the country, especially at dawn and dusk, you should proceed at a slower speed in case an animal jumps in front of your car. Traveling at the slower speed increases the probability you will avoid hitting the animal. If, however, a collision is inevitable, you also have a higher likelihood of surviving the crash if you are driving at a slower speed.

- If you hit a deer or other large animal while driving your car, <u>do not</u> approach the animal. Often the animal will lie injured and appear to be dead. Once approached, the wounded animal will fight, causing severe injury to those nearby. Leave the animal alone and call 911. Wait for the authorities.

To illustrate the above points, I was stationed at a rural facility where the wildlife and the humans interacted and coexisted. During mating season, the deer were everywhere on the roads. It was always a dangerous time for drivers, and we had 3 to 5 incidents per year. One day a friend of mine left the base after work about 6:00 p.m. in his red Miata. It was fall and beginning to get cold. The road had no streetlights and only an occasional farmhouse set back in the distance.

My friend, a Vietnam-era SEAL, was about half way to the main road when a large buck darted out in front of his car. Having no time to stop or slow down, he hit the deer broadside going 60 mph. Because of the low profile of the Miata, the deer slid up the hood and crashed through the windshield of the little car. He swerved into a ditch where the car came to a stop. The impact did not kill the deer immediately, but it was severely injured and afraid. Shaken up by the accident, my friend found himself in the cockpit of the Miata with a 300-pound deer and its antlers. He tried to get the door open with the buck kicking and flailing inside the small compartment. The whole ordeal lasted less than 15 seconds before he could get the car door open. However, in those 15 seconds, the buck kicked and mauled him until he was an unrecognizable, bloody mess. He lay in the ditch bleeding and semi-conscious for more than an hour before someone found him. He was gored twice with the antlers and all his ribs were either bruised or broken. He sustained a concussion and multiple lacerations from hitting the windshield. The buck finally died inside the Miata. Although my friend recovered, the car was totaled. In the end, this story is a reminder of how quickly disaster can strike.

Vehicle Safety Etiquette

You are most vulnerable to a carjacking when you unlock your doors to get out and before you lock your doors when you get into your car. As soon as you get into your vehicle, manually lock your doors, then get organized, and prepare to drive off. Do not wait for the automatic locks to engage. When entering or exiting your vehicle, be prepared to defend yourself. Keep your focus and be attentive at all times.

When you stop for gas, lock your car and ensure your valuables, including your computer, phone, and purse, are out of sight. The following scenarios describe crimes familiar to many.

- You make a quick stop at the gas station. As you fill your tank with gas, you are daydreaming. A stranger runs up to the car, opens the door, and grabs your purse, briefcase, cell phone, and whatever else is handy and runs away. The theft takes place so quickly many victims report never seeing the person well enough even to identify his or her race.

- A predator opens an unlocked door or smashes a window and grabs whatever is handy while the car owner is inside a gas station or convenience market. It is common, after all, to go inside to pay for gas and include a trip to the restroom and a walk around the store to look for something to eat. The theft can happen in the blink of an eye.

When parking your car, look for the safest locations possible. Well-lighted areas of the parking lot closest to your entrance are best. If you can park directly under a light, that is even better. Remember, when you go to work or the mall, you may arrive during the day but leave after dark. Consider a parking location based on the worst-case scenario—late at night when it is dark and not busy. If possible, you should always look for high-traffic and well-lit areas. When parking in a parking garage, find a parking space close to the door or the elevator. Keep in mind; isolation is an invitation to a predator. Getting you separated from the herd is the predator's primary goal. After that, the predator's job is easy.

In the event you are subject to a carjacking, your primary objective is not to be trapped inside the vehicle with the predator. Give up the car and your money and fight to stay out of the vehicle. If a predator forces you into your trunk, the good news is you are safer there than in the passenger area with an armed predator, and you have a way to get out. In all modern cars, there is an emergency escape handle in the trunk. Familiarize yourself with its location and operation on each of your vehicles. The emergency exit handle works regardless of whether the car is locked.

Emergency Contact Plans

Ensure that you have an emergency contact plan before you hit the road. Know what you are going to do if you have a flat tire or a mechanical issue. Have someone in mind to call whom you trust and is available. An emergency, whether a crash or a mechanical problem, often brings about stressful circumstances, and you do not want to have to figure out what to do under stress. The best case is to react according to a plan established under calm circumstances.

You should keep a written list of all your important phone numbers in the glove box with your license and registration. Why? Because invariably when you need a phone number in an emergency, your cell phone's battery will be dead and all your contacts will be locked securely inside the phone. Keep a phone charger in the car at all times. Have more than one contact for emergencies in the event your first choice (e.g., tow truck, friend, or family) is not available. ALWAYS have a PACE plan.

Primary Plan - Alternate Plan - Contingency Plan - Emergency Plan

REFINED AREAS OF VULNERABILITY
Outside the Home

Use the following checklist to break down the broad area of activities outside your home into sub-systems or vulnerabilities.

Identify those things that are vulnerable to attack:
- ☐ Mode of transportation
- ☐ Car computer
- ☐ Credit cards
- ☐ Important documents
- ☐ Social gatherings
- ☐ Appearance and profile
- ☐ Hotel room
- ☐ Rental car
- ☐ Air travel
- ☐ _____

Identify those things that you are vulnerable to:
- ☐ Traffic stops/Police encounters
- ☐ Carjacking
- ☐ Road rage
- ☐ Theft of valuables
- ☐ Mechanical trouble
- ☐ Accidents
- ☐ Theft
- ☐ _____

PDD™ CHECKLIST
Outside the Home

Now that you understand some of the vulnerabilities and risk mitigation options regarding vulnerabilities outside the home, use the following checklist to begin developing your security posture.

Prevention: What can you do to prevent becoming a target?
- ☐ Leave copies of your passport and other important documents with someone at home
- ☐ Carry a zip-up bag or purse
- ☐ Hook your backpack or purse around a table or chair when seated in public; never leave bags unattended or with a stranger
- ☐ Use ATMs only in protected environments
- ☐ Never leave your food or drink alone or with a stranger
- ☐ Travel to and from social events with a buddy
- ☐ Do not discuss more than superficial details of your job and life; have a cover story for people you don't know
- ☐ Dress appropriately for your environment
- ☐ Avoid the "James Bond" syndrome
- ☐ Keep the inside of your vehicle tidy and free of PII; leave nothing in the car to identify you
- ☐ Lock valuables in the trunk
- ☐ Maintain your vehicle properly
- ☐ Be aware of your surroundings at all times; have no distractions
- ☐ Park your car yourself; do not use a valet service; park in a safe location
- ☐ _____

Deterrence: What can you do to deter an attack once you become a target?
- ☐ Use an ankle or neck wallet for emergency stash, credit cards, important papers, and cash
- ☐ Keep an emergency survival kit with you when traveling
- ☐ Keep valuables and two days of clothing in a carry-on bag or go bag when flying
- ☐ Lock your doors immediately upon entry and exit of your vehicle
- ☐ Conduct yourself appropriately during traffic stops and police encounters on the streets

- ☐ Have a primary and emergency communications plan for accidents, mechanical issues, or other emergencies
- ☐ Know your state's roadside assistance phone number
- ☐ Have roadside assistance insurance
- ☐ Be prepared to evacuate your hotel room or any location or business you may be visiting at all times
- ☐ _____

Defense: What can you do if you are attacked?

- ☐ Be prepared to use your panic alarm when moving to and from the car and have your keys available as a weapon when moving to and from your car
- ☐ Don't get out of your car if threatened; use your car as a weapon if necessary
- ☐ Have a self-defense tool in the vehicle, ready to deploy (e.g., pepper spray, knife, club)
- ☐ Have a knife and window break tool handy from the driver's seat in the event of an accident
- ☐ Make an inventory of your valuables in the event of theft
- ☐ Know the location and phone number of the local U.S. Embassy if traveling abroad
- ☐ Know the emergency cell number to the highway patrol where you are traveling
- ☐ Be prepared for a physical attack; take a self-defense course
- ☐ _____

10 CHILD SAFETY

This section is not about parenting, but is intended to provide security recommendations for safeguarding your children from themselves, and more importantly, from others we allow into their world. It is impossible to cover every possible situation where a child may be endangered as that list would be long enough to warrant a dedicated book on the topic. The intent is not to focus on the obvious like child-proofing your home or the need to use an approved car seat, but instead to explore issues that have received less coverage but are infinitely more dangerous.

Daycare

Many parents with young children have to work and consequently, rely on daycare and after school programs to help manage their busy lives. While price and location are key criteria in choosing a childcare provider, other significant factors should be considered or at least evaluated in the process.

You should inquire as to whether the provider performs background checks on their employees. Make sure you understand what the provider considers having passed a background check. There is nothing wrong with asking about whether all of their staff have had, and passed background checks. Ask the provider specifically if the background check includes a search of the sexual offender registry and police records. For public awareness, most states provide online data with the names, recent photos, and work and home addresses, by zip code, of those convicted of sex crimes. Each state has different laws governing daycare facilities and not all require background checks.

Visit the facility unannounced and speak directly to the caregivers. Look for healthy personal habits like hygiene, grooming, and dress. How one treats themselves can often be a reflection of how they treat others. Talk to the staff about the facility, about how they came to that particular line of work, and bring up random topics not associated with child care. Observe their demeanor. Are the staff even tempered, patient, and well-mannered? Trust your instincts!

It is also helpful to look at the facility's features and attributes, so consider things such as management, staffing levels, security cameras, controlled access into and out of the facility, building layout for emergencies, and so forth. Managers set and control the culture. If the manager isn't professional and knowledgeable, then don't expect much from the staff. What you are doing is a vulnerability assessment and subsequent security plan before you commit to leaving your child in the hands of a stranger.

Security cameras can be a major safety feature. Studies have proven that behavior changes for the positive when employees know they are being observed. The presence of working security cameras that cover the facility at large and the rooms where the children spend most of their time is essential to promoting a safe environment. They serve as a deterrent and provide a record of who had access to a given room should anything happen. Cameras covering entry points should be positioned in such a way to capture the face of the person coming into the facility. Many businesses mount cameras on the ceiling, but these are less helpful unless there is something unique about the top of one's head.

Hiring a Nanny, Adult-aged Babysitter or Caregiver

Hiring an in-home nanny or adult-aged babysitter can be a great alternative to daycare and often provides a better experience for your child. However, when you hire in-home child care, you are assuming the responsibility of an employer with all the associated risks.

If you desire to do a background check on a nanny or adult babysitter, you are legally required under the Fair Credit Reporting Act to have their consent. Your prospective employee has the right to see and make a rebuttal to any derogatory information discovered. If you make a hiring decision not to select the person you must be prepared to defend your decision in the event they file suit.

It is best to seek out the services of a company specializing in background checks. These companies have people trained and experienced in sorting out the conflicting details associated with identity attributes and data sources needed to perform due diligence. Their services can generally be provided within a few days to a week and usually run a few hundred dollars. There is a base fee for the service, plus additional charges depending on the data you have them query (e.g., credit, criminal, bankruptcy, social media, etc.). The search can be tailored to your individual purpose, and the total cost is dependent upon the complexity of the background check.

You should have a prospective employee complete a formal job application which requires the disclosure of personal information because they are attesting and affirming that the information they provide is factual and accurate. Anything they omit or misrepresent can be the basis for non-selection and help protect you legally, especially if something concerning turns up on the background check. You want to make satisfactorily passing a background check a condition of employment.

It is an important distinction to note that companies offering instant background checks on the Internet do not typically provide analytical services. They will search public records and provide what is available for a fee. The value of this is not to be diminished as a useful and relatively inexpensive service. However, a company specializing in background checks takes the publicly available information and uses it as a foundation to further analyze an individual's life beyond what is accessible to the public.

It is unlikely that you will spend the money on due diligence when hiring a family member or friend you have known for some significant period. However, if you are considering leaving your child with a stranger for 6-8 hours a day at a significant hourly rate, then you should seriously consider thoroughly vetting anyone coming in contact with your children, family, or home. You are looking for negative patterns of behavior demonstrated in the candidate's past which could provide insight into their judgment and trustworthiness.

Similar to cameras in a daycare facility, having home security cameras when employing a nanny or any domestic help can be a significant deterrent to bad behavior. Additionally, cameras inside the home can provide insight into the quality of care, behavior, and demeanor of those whom you have entrusted to watch over your most cherished assets. You should have a paragraph in any employment agreement where your employee must consent to electronic monitoring by video and audio recording devices as a condition of employment. This can help protect you from the risk of frivolous litigation. You must use good judgment on when and where to utilize electronic monitoring as the right to privacy is based on "a reasonable expectation of privacy". This standard is somewhat subjective, but consider where you would want and expect privacy if the roles were reversed. If the answer is not clear, then you probably should seek professional advice when using electronic monitoring.

Everything in this section applies whether you are hiring a nanny or a caregiver for elderly parents or a child or adult with special needs.

Internet, Smart Phones, and Apps

One of most profound technocultural transformations of the past 20 years is the evolution of the mobile phone into a smartphone. Today's smartphones are reported to have the same computing power as the early space program computers that guided us to space and the moon. That capability, combined with the simultaneous maturation of the Internet as a communications technology, provides a platform of tremendous capability for a child, especially the teenage ones. Data, whether text or video, can travel around the world at the speed of light. What does this mean in the hands of your child?

It means your child has nearly an unlimited resource of knowledge with access to the world's great works of art and literature, insight into foreign cultures, and the opportunity to see the world in the palm of their hand. It provides a way for children to connect with each other and to communicate, socialize, and work homework virtually. However, it also means that the predator has unprecedented access to your child's data, thoughts, and vulnerabilities. It is up to you, not your child/teen, to provide a safe environment whether physically or virtually. We can all fall prey to scams and conmen. How much more vulnerable is your child? You must teach them, but you must vigilantly monitor and verify as well.

It was not that long ago when a child was on the wrong path, chose the wrong friends, or acted badly; parents would tell them "you can't play with Johnny because Johnny is a bad influence." Who your children played with was relatively easy to monitor and control. Today, however, pre-teens and teenagers reside and operate in a world most parents know very little about, much less who they are socializing and associating with online.

Children, whether pre-teens or teenagers, usually do not understand the dangers and risks associated with online exposure and maintaining an online presence. As a parent, you may think your child is busy in constructive pursuits simply because they may be sitting right there with you in the living room. We like to "assume" they are safe. Unfortunately, most parents don't have a good understanding of the complexities of the virtual world that is ubiquitous in a child's life today, so the assumption that they are safe is based on feeling and not fact.

Your son or daughter may think they made a new friend on social media because there is the photo of an attractive, smiling teenager who fits the persona of the dialogue. It cannot be overstated, nothing is as it appears on the Internet. Predators rely on the anonymity of the Internet to identify and gain access to the vulnerable. Some of these "new friends" might be other children we would never let our children play with, but in some cases, these new friends are not children at all. It is just a picture and a story. Just because you see it on the Internet does not make it true. We learn by experience. We learn that touching a hot plate or falling off a skateboard hurts. How do we teach our children about the dangers and risks of the Internet? Telling them a story doesn't carry the same learning opportunity as experience, so it doesn't have the same impact or carry the same danger signal as other experience-based learning.

Some popular apps on the market today provide the capability for people to make videos and post them online. Several of these apps have chat functions, which allow participants to communicate directly. Who are the people using the apps? In some cases, children as young as five years old have been seen posting videos on these video boards. There are a lot of pre-teens as well. If a song has a nice rhythm and sound, does that make it a nice song? Song content frequently gets by without close inspection and the same is true with these apps and their content.

You should not assume that a nicely packaged or visually appealing app is a safe playground for your children. If your child is a pre-teen or younger do they really need <u>unsupervised</u> access to a smartphone, tablet, or computer? Children learn very quickly how to manipulate and navigate applications and programs. They can switch between screens, conversations, and games so fast that it's hard to process what they are doing. They are trained from such a young age to multi-process large amounts of information that they can switch between programs while maintaining focus and context in all of them. There are new apps coming online every day that offers the predator ever-evolving opportunities to exploit the weak and uninformed. If you want your child to have online access, consider enabling controls that limit access. Enable age and content-appropriate apps, parental controls, and security settings such that your child cannot change or alter the settings to access inappropriate content.

While rare, there are plenty of horror stories where a predator targets a child on the Internet. Less rare and far more frequent is the exposure of children to inappropriate content. Over time this inappropriate content desensitizes them to violence, sexual conduct, drug use, and so on. You must be as vigilant in the virtual world as you are in the physical world when creating a safe environment for your children.

Your child's online activity, social media accounts, and exposure of personal information (e.g., birthday, school, etc.), all creates an opportunity for the predator. If you allow your child to have use of these apps, then you should control the information they put online. All of the things you do to protect yourself should, by extension, be imposed on your children. They should not expose too much personal information, reveal travel plans, or post any revealing or compromising pictures. As a child, overexposure makes you an easy target for a predator. As a parent, you should carefully review and understand the privacy settings for all social media accounts that your child is using. You can limit what others can see, who can contact your children, and what is exposed in the account. Social media is a great way for families to stay in touch and share pictures of events. Set your privacy settings such that what your child posts is only visible by those you know and trust. Consider the worst case of what someone could do knowing a few background facts about your child from their profile and page--your child's current photo, school, extra-curricular activities, names and pictures of their friends, your name (with a little research where you work), and so on. Does the world need to know your child is getting ice cream at the local ice cream parlor or riding their bike on Main Street at any given moment in time? The only way to remotely protect you child in the virtual world is to take control of their Internet use and regulate it like you would any other aspect of your child's life. Your child can have all the benefits of learning and using technology in a safe environment if you maintain some simple rules over what they can access. You can't necessarily control what they will do, but you can certainly control what they have access to and where they can expose themselves.

For young children and pre-teens, enabling parental controls is recommended regardless of whether it is a smartphone, tablet or computer. Having full visibility on a teenager is difficult. You'll be hard pressed to know what they are doing all of the time, but you can maintain awareness, which can help indicate emerging issues. There are a variety of products on the market which allow you to monitor or control your child's activities online.

A very helpful program is an "App Locker". There are several versions available in the various app stores, and there will inevitably be others coming on the market. An app locker is a program where you can identify specific apps on a phone or computer that you want to be hidden behind a separate authentication screen. For example, you may identify the "Play Store" and "Phone Settings" as two applications you want to have to authenticate with an additional password before accessing. In this case, your child can use the phone as designed to text, etc., however, if they try to access the "Play Store" or "Phone Settings" where they could change the call block list, they are met with an authentication screen where they must have the password to continue. This way you can control what your child can access based on trust limits.

Before you begin indiscriminately monitoring your child's online activities, there are a few things to consider. First, you need to own the phone or computer, and any cellular or data service for the phone needs to be in your name. Otherwise, you could be construed as in violation of electronic eavesdropping laws, so don't leave it open to interpretation. For example, if your child's phone is in your ex-spouse's name you have no right to monitor the phone regardless of whether you have custody of your child. Second, you are a parent, not a buddy, make no apologies. As a minor, there is no right to privacy on the phone. There may be an expectation of privacy but no right to privacy. Everything they do online is in the public domain, so they should assume everything they do online is in the public eye. They need to understand that you as a parent are always monitoring their activities as well. Your children should understand that if it is not something they would say or do in front of the world, then they shouldn't do it online either.

Spyware or monitoring programs are usually by subscription and discounted for longer term service agreements. Do your research, look at the ratings and number of reviews, then read the reviews from people who have used a particular service. Before getting into a long-term agreement, try out the product for a month to see if it is intuitive and provides the insight you are seeking to achieve.

For smartphones, there is a lot of talk about jailbreaking a phone. OEM operating systems were designed to run on the phones in the manner they were engineered. When you jailbreak a phone, you change the operating system and creating new vulnerabilities. So, let's define the terms.

Jailbreaking is the process of bypassing digital rights restrictions on IOS devices to install other apps and programs not approved by Apple. *Rooting* is a similar process but is the hacking of Android devices, game consoles, and so on. "Rooting" and "jailbreaking" are often used interchangeably when talking about mobile devices. Bottom line, jailbreaking and rooting a device is a mechanism to bypass inherent security features and provide access to unvetted apps and programs. Once you jailbreak or root a phone, you have created immeasurable vulnerabilities unless you are a seasoned software aficionado which few of us are.

Find a spyware or monitoring program with the features you desire that does not jailbreak the phone and degrade the security features built into the OEM programming. Monitoring apps and programs can be a significant enabler in defending your child from predators on the Internet but don't make the phone more vulnerable in the process.

There are two approaches to managing your child's perception of spyware on a phone or computer. The first is an entirely covert approach. You own the phone and computer so you can install whatever monitoring programs you choose and covertly monitor your child's activities. The second approach is to be overt about the whole process. Let your child know they are being monitored and what the limitations are. There are positives and negatives associated with each. If your child ever discovers they are being covertly monitored, there is a significant degradation in trust. Conversely, if you let your child know they are being monitored they can quickly find workarounds for almost any monitoring effort.

Regardless of your approach, you'll know a lot more about your teen if you monitor their activity. In some cases, it may be more than you wanted to know, but it is necessary information in the ongoing effort of protecting your child.

Instilling good Internet behavior is a lesson your child can carry over into adult life and practices. Colleges now include social media background checks in the admissions process as a way to reduce liability and the potential for future problems. Future employers also do background and social media checks to determine a prospective employee's judgment when publicly sharing data, photos, videos, postings, etc. They use this information to make hiring decisions, and it is based on character and ethics. Some teens (and adults) have learned the hard way that you can't say anything you want on the Internet free of consequence. Derogatory social media posts about an employer have led to adverse actions and employment terminations. Begin to instill safe Internet behavior from the outset of your child's use of the web and it will serve them well in the future.

Teen Driving

Learning to drive brings a sense of power, freedom, and recognition for a teenager. A learner's permit and driver's license are milestones in the lives of your teen. No doubt they revel in the freedom and so do you. Your teen is growing up and moving towards adulthood and independence.

However, driving is a privilege, and it comes with the responsibility to act appropriately and demonstrate good judgment. Irresponsible behavior brings accountability and loss of privilege. You may consider a cell phone app that blocks texting and calling while driving. These apps use the accelerometer on the phone to determine when the phone is moving and then disable texting and calling functionality until the vehicle has stopped.

You can research these on Google Play or iTunes. These are good alternatives to more intrusive means of behavior control.

Insurance companies now offer a device that can be plugged into a vehicle which monitors location, speed, and braking. These devices are marketed as a safety measure that can save you money on your insurance. The implication is that as it monitors your driving habits, you get some monetary consideration on your insurance for safe driving behavior. At first glance, you may think this is an excellent idea and because you are a very safe driver this will ultimately save you money. The truth, in fact, is that anything collected from this device and stored with the insurance agency is up for interpretation by the agency and is vulnerable in a subpoena. That data is also only as secure as the agency's privacy policies. Consider the eventuality that the agency sells your driving data, which is very likely at some point in time.

You must consider the fact that you want and need to keep track of your teenager, but you do not necessarily want to expose them to the world in your attempt to keep them safe. You, as a parent, can be as detrimental to your teen's reputation as they can without careful consideration of your actions. Anything that looks appealing as a safety measure, such as the aforementioned, should be carefully evaluated before buying in.

The Nuclear Option

So what do you do when you inevitably discover your child is smarter than you are? When you realize, at 45 years old, it is unlikely you fully grasp the digital world your child lives in or the threats it poses to them every day. The digital world changes and evolves as new apps and techniques are exposed. So, no matter how savvy you think you are, your teen, and technology is a step or generation ahead. It is simply the truth based on how rapidly technology is evolving and how fast children process information.

An alternative approach is to disrupt and deconstruct the layers of complexity your teen builds on their devices over time by kicking over the anthill and making them start over. A couple of actions to illustrate the point: do a factory reset of your child's devices (like a brand new device from the store with no loaded data or apps), and cancel any credit cards they use to procure online services. The objective is to break their contact with the virtual world and make it extremely hard to rebuild their layered online infrastructure.

This nuclear option may be something you only use once to break a bad habit, or it may be something that you explicitly state happens every two weeks, 60 days, etc., whatever is appropriate. The objective is to make it technically difficult for your teen to continue to rebuild and create bad relationships. The reason this works is your child will have to reinitialize every social media app, game, etc. All photos and files stored on the phone or computer will be lost. Often they will need to set up new accounts with some of the providers, and this can be time-consuming. Of course, over the long term, if your teen is unwilling to change behavior nothing you do technically is going to affect the outcome. You are only trying to gain insight and limit exposure in an already bad circumstance.

There is a fine line you are balancing whenever you invoke monitoring or destruction techniques. Monitoring is the most effective. There are software tools available that monitor all activity on a phone or computer so it becomes very difficult for your child to use the latest communication apps to prevent you from discovering their activities. However, that level of monitoring is difficult to sustain covertly, and your teen is going to feel an extreme violation of privacy because they have no private place to go online and be a teenager. When you factory reset a device you push your child to find online or cloud resources where they can interact with others and store their data.

Take, for example, computers that have very little onboard memory storage like the Chromebook. In this case factory resetting the device does nothing because the user does everything online in the cloud. The intent of these devices is to push the user down a path where data and apps are no longer stored locally but rather are ubiquitously available, agnostic to your access device. Services and providers store the data for you. Consequently, you can access the data from any device whether the device is yours or not. As a parent, this is difficult for you to monitor or defeat. However, there are always options.

What do you look for and monitor whether physically looking at the phone or technically monitoring the phone or computer? Break it down to what is really of concern. These aren't going to change. How your child gains access is what changes.

- Browsing history – what websites is your child visiting?

- Apps downloaded on the device – what private gaming or communications apps have been downloaded on the device. The app provides the portal to the Internet whether anything is stored on the device or not. Some apps have built-in Instant Messaging (IM) or chat functions, so look beyond the obvious purpose of the app to other functions and make a conscious decision whether to accept the risks or not. Some apps, will by default, have the microphone and camera activated. For these, consider whether the functions are truly needed to serve its intended purpose. If not, then turn those features off.

- Call log – Who is you communicating with your child? If you do not recognize the name in the call log, you should do an Internet search of the number. Often teens will use false names in their contacts list for those individuals they know you would disapprove of to mask the activity. During the service month, many providers list the calls by date, time, and the number called or received. Regular monitoring of the call history on your bill will highlight activity of concern and will appear regardless of deletions from the device.

- Text log – Outside of encrypted communications apps, the basic texting log of the device is the most valuable. Most of us, teens especially, prefer texting as the base communications method. They are far more likely to text than talk on the phone. For the same reasons as explained in the Call Log, pay particular attention to the contact names.

All of this seems extreme for your wonderful child that is beyond reproach and is likely to be the next President of the United States, right? Remember, your child can be as well-meaning and honest as the day is long, but there are predators out there who seek to coach the well-meaning, inexperienced, and vulnerable into doing things they would otherwise never do. These strategies involve incremental changes leading to significant risk and danger. Convincing your child they should use a particular app to communicate, "because [their] parents just wouldn't understand," is part of the process of moving your child in the direction desired by the predator. It develops a trust between the predator and child and creates a false sense of security in that the parents won't find out and what harm can come from texting. There are a thousand ways to manipulate that conversation, but the fundamentals of what you as a parent should look for never change.

Remember, don't get forced down the path of trying to keep up with your child technically, this is time-consuming and becoming increasingly difficult. Identify what you need to know to keep your child safe and impose rules that provide you the necessary information regardless of technological changes.

AREA OF VULNERABILITY
Child Safety

Use the following checklist to break down the broad area of child safety into sub-systems or vulnerabilities.

Identify those things in your child's life where they are vulnerable to attack:

- ☐ Internet browsing habits
- ☐ Social media accounts
- ☐ Others that tag your child on social media
- ☐ PII
- ☐ Reputation
- ☐ Data storage
- ☐ _____

Identify those things that your child is vulnerable to:

- ☐ Day care personnel
- ☐ Nanny/babysitter
- ☐ Over exposure, physically or virtually
- ☐ Internet Predators
- ☐ Bullying
- ☐ _____

PDD™ CHECKLIST
Child Safety

Now that you understand some of the vulnerabilities and risk mitigation options regarding your child's safety, use the following checklist to begin developing your security posture. Much of protecting a child falls in the Prevention phase.

Prevention: What can you do to prevent your child from becoming a target?
- ☐ Have background checks done for anyone caring for your child
- ☐ Use nanny cameras for situational awareness
- ☐ Conduct surprise visits on anyone caring for your child, this includes school
- ☐ Monitor your child's phone and computer regularly, this includes social media
- ☐ Carry liability insurance if you have an in-home caregiver
- ☐ Use an app locker on all devices to restrict your child's access to things like the play store and call blocking
- ☐ Don't let you child jailbreak their phone
- ☐ Impose parental controls on phones and computers
- ☐ Ensure you have full device access
- ☐ Ensure YOU own all of your child's devices and accounts
- ☐ Run a good antivirus on all your child's devices
- ☐ Don't expose your child's PII on social media
- ☐ Employ a cell phone app that blocks texting and calling while driving
- ☐ _____

Deterrence: What can you do to deter an attack once your child becomes a target?
- ☐ Trace suspect phone numbers
- ☐ Block suspect phone numbers from calling or texting
- ☐ Report predators and bullies
- ☐ _____

Defense: What can you do if you are attacked?
- ☐ Factory reset the phone or computer
- ☐ Break contact and take the phone away
- ☐ _____

11 PDD™ CHECKLISTS

Use the checklists in this chapter to evaluate and reevaluate your security posture. Look at your life holistically and be vigilant. Build your list of areas where you need to focus and continue to refine your security posture as your life and circumstances change over time.

AREA OF VULNERABILITY
Personally Identifiable Information

Use the following checklist to break down the broad area of personally identifiable information into sub-systems or vulnerabilities.

Identify those areas of PII that are vulnerable to attack:
- ☐ Purchase patterns
- ☐ Financial data
- ☐ Medical data
- ☐ _____

Identify those things you are vulnerable to:
- ☐ Telemarketing solicitations
- ☐ Email scams
- ☐ Office theft
- ☐ Data breaches at credit card companies, retailers, hospitals, and others
- ☐ Aggregation of your data
- ☐ _____

PDD™ CHECKLIST
Personally Identifiable Information

Now that you understand some of the vulnerabilities and risk mitigation options regarding personally identifiable information, use the following checklist to begin developing your security posture.

Prevention: What can you do to prevent becoming a target?
- ☐ Shred all paperwork containing PII
- ☐ Subscribe to a fraud alert program
- ☐ Review your credit report every six months
- ☐ Permanently close old credit card accounts you no longer use and make closures irreversible
- ☐ Set fraud alerts on credit card and bank accounts
- ☐ Lock your computer when away
- ☐ Secure all PII at work and school in a locked cabinet or desk
- ☐ Don't use rewards cards or credit cards when purchasing sensitive medications
- ☐ _____

Deterrence: What can you do to deter an attack once you become a target?
- ☐ Do not provide any PII to anyone who calls you; verify only information the caller already has
- ☐ Never open a link sent to you in email or text unless you are sure it is legitimate
- ☐ Never provide PII over an unsecure or non-https:// web address
- ☐ Never send money to any solicitation or warning of inappropriate web searching
- ☐ _____

Defense: What can you do if you are attacked?
- ☐ Report suspicious activity to your fraud alert provider immediately
- ☐ If your credit or debit card has been compromised, ask the provider to close the cards and issue new ones
- ☐ Report evidence of mail fraud to the Postmaster General

☐ Block suspicious/phishing email addresses
☐ Report foreign email scams looking for money or personal information to the FBI
☐ _____

AREA OF VULNERABILITY
Communications Security
Computers, Phones, and Social Media

Use the following checklist to break down the broad area of communications security into sub-systems or vulnerabilities.

Identify those areas of communication that are vulnerable to attack:

- ☐ Computers and phones
- ☐ Unsecure Internet connections
- ☐ Cloud data storage
- ☐ Passwords
- ☐ Company-supplied phones and computers, BYOD apps
- ☐ Professional networking sites
- ☐ Personally Identifiable Information
- ☐ Online posts
- ☐ Internet surfing habits
- ☐ _____

Identify the things you are vulnerable to:

- ☐ Computer viruses
- ☐ Unsecure websites
- ☐ Software installs
- ☐ Cookies/Browser habits
- ☐ Cell phone applications
- ☐ Social media exploitation
- ☐ Selling of personal data
- ☐ Identity theft
- ☐ Financial fraud
- ☐ Cyberbullying
- ☐ _____

PDD™ CHECKLIST
Communications Security
Computers, Phones, and Social Media

Now that you understand some of the vulnerabilities and risk mitigation options regarding communications security, use the following checklist to begin developing your security posture.

Prevention: What can you do to prevent becoming a target?

☐ Install antivirus software on all your devices

☐ Use only secure https:// addresses when you send PII or shop online

☐ Research apps and software updates before installing

☐ Use a private browsing feature when surfing the Internet

☐ Never click on links from unknown or suspect addresses

☐ Never respond to "government warnings" of illicit behavior

☐ Back up your computer data

☐ Keep all PII out of the cloud

☐ Use only secure Wi-Fi networks

☐ Ensure home Wi-Fi is password protected

☐ Use strong passwords and change your passwords every 90 days

☐ Use a different password for every account

☐ Maintain a private cell phone and email account; don't conduct personal business on work-supplied cell phones or computers

☐ Understand your company's BYOD policies

☐ Do not loan your computer or phone to friends or acquaintances

☐ Be cautious about content you post online; think twice before hitting send; keep emails professional and void of rumor, innuendo, and defamation

☐ Use a fraud protection service

☐ _____

Deterrence: What can you do to deter an attack once you become a target?

☐ Monitor your online presence, bank accounts, and utilities for unusual activity at least monthly

☐ Report suspicious account activity immediately to the service provider

☐ Change passwords immediately upon discovery of suspicious activity

☐ Dispose of private phone numbers and email addresses upon discovery of suspicious activity (hacking)

☐ Change your Wi-Fi network password if you feel you have been compromised

☐ _____

Defense: What can you do if you are attacked?

☐ Have a tracking and self-destruct app on your cell phone and laptop

☐ Factory reset and properly dispose of old hardware, computers, and phones

☐ _____

AREA OF VULNERABILITY
The Home

Use the following checklist to break down the broad area of the home into subsystems or vulnerabilities.

Identify those things that are vulnerable to attack:
- ☐ Your profile
- ☐ Garbage
- ☐ Mail
- ☐ Wi-Fi
- ☐ Guns
- ☐ Your children
- ☐ _____

Identify those things that you are vulnerable to:
- ☐ Home invasion
- ☐ Fire
- ☐ Medical emergency
- ☐ Domestic help
- ☐ Heavy neighborhood crime
- ☐ _____

PDD™ CHECKLIST
The Home

Now that you understand some of the vulnerabilities and risk mitigation options regarding physical security in the home, use the following checklist to begin developing your security posture.

Prevention: What can you do to prevent becoming a target?
- ☐ Maintain a low profile
- ☐ Put only household garbage curbside
- ☐ Maintain an out-of-neighborhood mailbox for private communications
- ☐ Shred junk mail
- ☐ Shred all PII-related mail and documents
- ☐ Put a security alarm sign in your window or yard or both
- ☐ Have guest garage or alarm codes that expire
- ☐ Keep doors and windows locked at all times
- ☐ _____

Deterrence: What can you do to deter an attack once you become a target?
- ☐ Have a dog that barks
- ☐ Have an alarm system and use it
- ☐ Have a safe or fireproof lock box
- ☐ Secure your weapons
- ☐ Install external lighting
- ☐ Keep shrubs cut back
- ☐ Find a safe place to park
- ☐ Install cameras in/around the home
- ☐ Employ deception techniques to increase your defensive appearance
- ☐ _____

Defense: What can you do if you are attacked?
- ☐ Be prepared for a physical attack; take a self-defense course
- ☐ Keep weapons available throughout the house within easy reach
- ☐ Have a remote panic alarm for the house
- ☐ Have a rehearsed emergency plan for intrusion, fire, and medical emergency
- ☐ Place multiple fire extinguishers around the house

- ☐ Install smoke detectors in all bedrooms and the main living area
- ☐ Identify a safe room
- ☐ Have an evacuation kit available near your primary emergency exit
- ☐ _____

AREA OF VULNERABILITY
Outside the Home

Use the following checklist to break down the broad area of activities outside your home into sub-systems or vulnerabilities.

Identify those things that are vulnerable to attack:
- ☐ Mode of transportation
- ☐ Car computer
- ☐ Credit cards
- ☐ Important documents
- ☐ Social gatherings
- ☐ Appearance and profile
- ☐ Hotel room
- ☐ Rental car
- ☐ Air travel
- ☐ _____

Identify those things that you are vulnerable to:
- ☐ Traffic stops/Police encounters
- ☐ Carjacking
- ☐ Road rage
- ☐ Theft of valuables
- ☐ Mechanical trouble
- ☐ Accidents
- ☐ Theft
- ☐ _____

PDD™ CHECKLIST
Outside the Home

Now that you understand some of the vulnerabilities and risk mitigation options regarding vulnerabilities when outside the home, use the following checklist to begin developing your security posture.

Prevention: What can you do to prevent becoming a target?

- ☐ Leave copies of your passport and other important documents with someone at home
- ☐ Carry a zip-up bag or purse
- ☐ Hook your backpack or purse around a table or chair when seated in public; never leave bags unattended or with a stranger
- ☐ Use ATMs only in protected environments
- ☐ Never leave your food or drink alone or with a stranger
- ☐ Travel to and from social events with a buddy
- ☐ Do not discuss more than superficial details of your job and life; have a cover story for people you don't know
- ☐ Dress appropriately for your environment
- ☐ Avoid the "James Bond" syndrome
- ☐ Keep the inside of your vehicle tidy and free of PII; leave nothing in the car to identify you
- ☐ Lock valuables in the trunk
- ☐ Maintain your vehicle properly
- ☐ Be aware of your surroundings at all times; have no distractions
- ☐ Park your car yourself; do not use a valet service; park in a safe location
- ☐ _____

Deterrence: What can you do to deter an attack once you become a target?

- ☐ Use an ankle or neck wallet for emergency stash, credit cards, important papers, and cash
- ☐ Keep an emergency survival kit with you when traveling
- ☐ Keep valuables and two days of clothing in a carry-on bag or go bag when flying
- ☐ Lock your doors immediately upon entry and exit of your vehicle
- ☐ Conduct yourself appropriately during traffic stops and police encounters on the streets

☐ Have a primary and emergency communications plan for accidents, mechanical issues, or other emergencies

☐ Know your state's roadside assistance phone number

☐ Have roadside assistance insurance

☐ Be prepared to evacuate your hotel room or any location or business you may be visiting at all times

☐ _____

Defense: What can you do if you are attacked?

☐ Be prepared to use your panic alarm when moving to and from the car and have your keys available as a weapon when moving to and from your car

☐ Don't get out of your car if threatened; use your car as a weapon if necessary

☐ Have a self-defense tool in the vehicle, ready to deploy (e.g., pepper spray, knife, club)

☐ Have a knife and window break tool handy from the driver's seat in the event of an accident

☐ Make an inventory of your valuables in the event of theft

☐ Know the location and phone number of the local U.S. Embassy if traveling abroad

☐ Know the emergency cell number to the highway patrol where you are traveling

☐ Be prepared for a physical attack; take a self-defense course

☐ _____

AREA OF VULNERABILITY
Child Safety

Use the following checklist to break down the broad area of child safety into sub-systems or vulnerabilities.

Identify those things in your child's life where they are vulnerable to attack:
- ☐ Internet browsing habits
- ☐ Social media accounts
- ☐ Others that tag your child on social media
- ☐ PII
- ☐ Reputation
- ☐ Data storage
- ☐ _____

Identify those things that your child is vulnerable to:
- ☐ Day care personnel
- ☐ Nanny/babysitter
- ☐ Over exposure, physically or virtually
- ☐ Internet Predators
- ☐ Bullying
- ☐ _____

PDD™ CHECKLIST
Child Safety

Now that you understand some of the vulnerabilities and risk mitigation options regarding your child's safety, use the following checklist to begin developing your security posture. Much of protecting a child falls in the Prevention phase.

Prevention: What can you do to prevent your child from becoming a target?
- ☐ Have background checks done for anyone caring for your child
- ☐ Use nanny cameras for situational awareness
- ☐ Conduct surprise visits on anyone caring for your child, this includes school
- ☐ Monitor your child's phone and computer regularly, this includes social media
- ☐ Carry liability insurance if you have an in-home caregiver
- ☐ Use an app locker on all devices to restrict your child's access to things like the play store and call blocking
- ☐ Don't let you child jailbreak their phone
- ☐ Impose parental controls on phones and computers
- ☐ Ensure you have full device access
- ☐ Ensure YOU own all of your child's devices and accounts
- ☐ Run a good antivirus on all your child's devices
- ☐ Don't expose your child's PII on social media
- ☐ Employ a cell phone app that blocks texting and calling while driving
- ☐ _____

Deterrence: What can you do to deter an attack once your child becomes a target?
- ☐ Trace suspect phone numbers
- ☐ Block suspect phone numbers from calling or texting
- ☐ Report predators and bullies
- ☐ _____

Defense: What can you do if you are attacked?
- ☐ Factory reset the phone or computer
- ☐ Break contact and take the phone away
- ☐ _____

EPILOGUE

Beware the Predator is an easy-to-read guide for individuals who want to raise their security awareness and protect themselves and their organizations from being targeted by criminal predators or corporate or state spying. If you are a corporate or government executive, a high-net-worth individual, or someone concerned about identity theft, then you should be concerned about your safety and the vulnerability of your personal data. What are you willing to spend to protect yourself? What is your organization willing to pay to defend itself? This book provides practical ways to reduce your personal exposure and mitigate your risks. It gives ideas how to make yourself and your employees a harder target to exploit. Beware the Predator will help you strengthen your security program, enhance protection of data you wish to keep secret, and generate a bigger return on investment for your organization.

Most people are not spies and do not think like spies, nor do they think of themselves as targets for crime or data collection. They can understand a robbery or similar crime in terms of motivation, opportunity, and intent, but use and theft of their data is a more ambiguous and disconnected concept. The thought process usually is as follows: "Why would anybody care about me or my data?" The truth is that what we have—our identity, history, and what we know—all have value to someone.

Data collection on individuals, groups, and organizations happens every minute of every day. It happens for a host of legitimate purposes, such as marketing products to consumers or functional reasons like managing healthcare and government programs. However, there are those who seek to collect data with their own goals and ends in mind. These individuals frequently are linked to enabling criminal activities like stealing identity data and attributes or compromising an organization's computer network.

Security is only as good as the weakest link in the chain of defense. Whether they realize it or not, for an organization, security doesn't start when you walk in the door at work. We all have patterns of behavior that can be vulnerable and exploited. This causes the line between an employee and employer and our personal and professional lives to blur where the two intersect and overlap, such as the passwords you make up and use to access your computer network accounts.

When does behavior cause our data to become vulnerable? In our daily lives, we freely use our credit cards, smart phones, computers, electronic accounts, apps, and a host of other things that are supposed to make our lives better, more efficient, and more networked and interconnected than ever before. We expand our social network in some cases to persons we have never met. We articulate our thoughts, lifestyle, issues, ideologies, and the causes we support. We manage our finances online. In doing so, we create a digital footprint with every credit card swipe, every traffic camera we pass, each app we activate on our phone or computer, and every single post or "like" on social networking without fully considering the risks.

These data points might seem overwhelming to an individual who might be trying to sort and analyze them all. However, by using sophisticated software and powerful computers to do the heavy lifting, this work can be done relatively easily. Every week or two, news breaks of a business or government agency that has their computer networks hacked; business or mission disrupted; and personal, business, and mission data compromised.

If you are an officer of a corporation, executive in government, a high-net-worth individual, or someone who has reason to be concerned about personal security (to include identity theft), then you need to read Beware the Predator. Watch for future offerings on cyber security and identity theft topics from Mockingbird Security and Spartan Security Consulting, LLC.

Dave White, Washington, D.C.

ABOUT THE AUTHOR

As a career Technical Operations Officer, Mr. Warren Holston has worked throughout the Intelligence Community, Department of Defense, and defense industry for more than 30 years. He has served as a U.S. Navy Explosive Ordnance Disposal Diver, a collection officer and senior manager in the Central Intelligence Agency, and a Subject Matter Expert for the Department of Defense U.S. Special Operations Command. Mr. Holston has managed and conducted counterterrorism, covert action, and technical collection operations worldwide and is recognized as having contributed significantly to the national security of the United States of America. He was awarded the CIA's Intelligence Commendation Medal for "conceiving of, and implementing, a clandestine sensor operation against a high priority denied area intelligence target" and the Distinguished Career Intelligence Medal for "superior performance in the conduct of clandestine operations in the CIA."

AMBASSADOR COFER BLACK

Ambassador Cofer Black is an internationally acknowledged, 30-year career, U.S. government leader and expert in counterterrorism and national security. During 2002–2005, at the Assistant Secretary of State level, he reported to the Secretary of State for developing, coordinating, and implementing American counterterrorism policy. He served a 28-year career at CIA, reaching Senior Intelligence Service (SIS-4) level as Director, Counterterrorist Center (D/CTC) during the 9/11 period, including launching the response against Al-Qaeda in Afghanistan and worldwide.

He completed six successful operational CIA tours abroad in field management positions focusing on counterterrorism and addressed regional security, counterintelligence, and covert action issues. His awards include the Distinguished Intelligence Medal, the highest award for performance; the Distinguished Career Intelligence Medal; the Donovan Award; as well as the Exceptional Collector Award for 1994, among others. He served as Special Advisor on foreign policy to Governor Mitt Romney during his 2008 and 2012 Presidential election campaigns. Ambassador Black earned B.A. and M.A. degrees in International Relations from the University of Southern California.

MR. DAVE WHITE

Mr. White has worked for the U.S. government in a broad range of roles and missions within the Intelligence and Defense Communities for almost 30 years. He has extensive leadership, systems engineering, and intelligence analysis and operations experience.

Mr. White served in the U.S. Air Force for 20 years. He began his career in the enlisted ranks of the U.S. Air Force, earned a commission, and retired as a Lieutenant Colonel-select. He has directed and managed imagery and signals collection operations on sensitive U.S. government platforms and led a variety of intelligence analysis units focused on delivering national security products to operators and policymakers.

Since his retirement from the Air Force, Mr. White has focused on identity intelligence, biometrics, behavioral analysis, and biographical data. He has served as a Deputy Senior Operations Officer and Identity Intelligence Analyst at the National Counterterrorism Center (NCTC) and as a biometrics technology consultant in the Intelligence Community.

Mr. White has supported activities in the Defense Intelligence Agency (DIA), National Security Agency (NSA), National Geospatial-Intelligence Agency (NGA), Office of the Director of National Intelligence (ODNI), and Air Force Intelligence. He has been a guest speaker at the CIA's Sherman Kent School for Intelligence Analysis, Department of Defense's Joint Special Operations University, and National Signatures Symposium. Mr. White is the CEO, Spartan Security Consulting, LLC, which specializes in identity intelligence, management, and services. Spartan was founded in 2014 in Herndon, Virginia.

Made in the USA
San Bernardino, CA
17 March 2017